ABORTION

ANALYZING OLD & NEW ARGUMENTS

Dr. Robert O'Connor

Total Health Publications

2019

THE AUTHOR

Bob O'Connor is a retired professor who obtained his doctorate in the philosophy of education from the University of Southern California with an emphasis on political theory, ethics, and religion. He is also a licensed Marriage, Family and Child Counsellor in California. He has taught philosophy and ethics as well as health education, including marriage and family issues, including parenting.

ACKNOWLEDGEMENTS

A hearty "thank you" to my clients, students, friends, and acquaintances, who have forced me to think more deeply about the issue concerning this topic. The pros and cons, the present and the future, the joys and sorrows of parenthood—are among the questions and concerns of many of the youth and mature citizens. It is not a simple proposition. Strongly felt needs and the counterbalancing traditions—make abortion a complicated ethical and moral hot potato. I hope I have clarified some of the options.

And a special thanks to Hanne Overlier for editing the text and suggesting many useful avenues to address and pursue.

ABLE OF CONTENTS

CHAPTER I—INTRODUCTION TO ABORTION—SOME ARGUMENTS PRO AND CON

Nearly 54 percent of black women reported an unintended pregnancy, compared with 43 percent of Hispanic women, and about 31 percent of white women. How many might think they are not ready for parenthood when this pregnancy "*appeared*?"

WHAT IF—???

A woman whose religious views makes it clear that she will not terminate the pregnancy under any circumstances. However, the Angel Gabriel felt obliged to visit her. He told her that the life of her child, once born, would be that of a serial rapist-murderer, killing over a hundred people. Additionally, he would torture and kill all the members of her family. Would this persuade her to change her mind?

On the other side of town, an hour later, another pregnant woman, who had no qualms about aborting her embryo, was visited by the same busy angel. He told her that the embryo that she was intent on aborting would grow up to be a humanitarian and a loving person like Albert Schweitzer, and an intelligent and financially able person like Bill Gates--the world's greatest humanitarian, and the child would be a constant joy to her life. Would this persuade her to change her mind?

We all have opinions on which we lead our lives. Are we willing to change our minds as new and true information becomes available? After all-- a mind made up, ceases to exist! If we have a mind, it is to determine truth—not to rationalize groundless opinions.

FAITH

Much of what we do in life requires faith. We usually have faith that we will wake up tomorrow morning. More than 150,000 people a day are wrong in that faith. They woke up dead!

How many German and American women in 1928 thought that there would never be another world war? After all, the war to end all wars had been finished only 10 years earlier. But in another 10 years, the German woman would be involved in war preparations and in 15 years both the German and the Americans would be involved in a greater world war.

Faith is essential in our lives. But it is often wrong.

Do the anti-abortion people have faith that a pregnant alcoholic woman will not have a child born with fetal alcohol syndrome? Do they have faith that the heroin addicted mother will not give birth to an addicted child who will have to suffer the pains of withdrawal? Alcohol, opioids, cannabis, tobacco, cocaine, and many other drugs can have severe, often lifelong, effects on the embryo or fetus. West Virginia is the most heavily affected state from opioid abuse. At one hospital, Cabell Huntington Hospital, one in five newborns has been exposed to opioids in the womb.

Do they have faith that women, or their partners—if they have one-- will always be loving and caring for their children who were unwanted?

We tend to think that everyone thinks like we do. If I am a caring and loving mother, all women will think as I do. This is of course, absurd.

I remember a woman, in my practice who was severely neurotic. She had multiple personalities and satisfied her power drive by believing she was unusually holy. She wrote letters to priests and ministers whom she wanted to follow her. None of them answered her. In one session, she brought a few friends and her adult daughter. One friend asked her if her religious beliefs were not secondary to the love of her daughter. She said that her beliefs were primary. Soon after, her daughter disowned her.

Many years earlier, the father of the child had divorced her. She didn't want the child, but he did. A neighbor, assuming that the mother had the same ability to love that she had, told her that she should have the child since she was the mother. It is quite common for people to hide their personality problems from acquaintances. And, of course, much of our belief system is based on our traditional beliefs, and what we see and hear. Then, we all have great faith that our beliefs are true.

At that time, as today, mothers usually get custody—and the mother did. About ten years later, other neighbors were exposed to the multiple personalities (St. Paul, a prostitute, and a housewife). They prevailed on her to give up her 14 year-old child, which she did. But there had been almost a decade of psychological and physical trauma that the daughter had to deal with. It took years of counselling to eliminate most of the effects of living with her neurotic mother.

It is unlikely that any of you readers have such a strong neurotic faith. You may not be able to understand how a mother can place her daughter in such a secondary role. You may not also understand how a terrorist can drive a truck down a crowded roadway with the intent on killing and injuring as many people as possible. This idea does not "compute" for most of us.

Most American readers would not understand the principles of Buddha. So, would not have much faith in his principles. Most people in Thailand would not understand the religions of Abraham, so would not put much stock in them. But they would believe the principles of Buddhism. So, the origins of our faiths are generally based on the traditions of our geographical placement. Being born and bred in a farm in Iowa will probably give you quite different aspects of your faith than if you were born in a ghetto in Los Angeles.

So, if we are to be intelligent about our views on abortion, we must realize how our opinions developed and that they may not be verifiable except in our limited experience.

WHO HOLDS WHAT OPINIONS?

According to a Pew report in October 2018, 58% of Americans believe that abortion should be legal in all or most cases, while 37% say should be illegal in all or most cases, these percentages have stayed relatively stable for 25 years. 61% of Evangelical Protestants said it should be illegal in most cases. 51% of Catholics think it should be legal in all or most cases, while 42% say it should be illegal in all or most cases. 59% of Republican respondents said it should be illegal in all or most cases, while 24% of Democrats say it should be illegal. 60% of women and 57% of men say it should be legal in all or most cases.

When we look at it from an educational perspective, 48% of those with high school educations approve of abortion, 63% of those with some college education and 71% of college graduates approve of it.

You might be interested in the educational backgrounds of people, in general, when looking at their abortion views. In the U.S., we find that Hindus have the highest level of college graduation at 77%. Unitarians are at 67%, Jews at 59%, Episcopalians at 56%, atheists at 43%, Muslims at 39% Mormons and Lutherans in the low 30s, Catholics at 26%, Baptists at 19%, and Jehovah's Witnesses at 12%.

These rates do not tell us the quality of the college education. Certainly, Harvard and the University of California rank much higher than most other universities. The highest rated schools with the backing of a religion are: Notre Dame at 18 and Pepperdine at 46. Many don't make the top 200, like Liberty University. So, college diplomas are not equal—in fact there can be huge differences in the knowledges of college graduates, depending on: the college, the academic level of the graduate, the college major, the quality of the professors, and the quality of extra-curricular activities, such as travelling.

We would certainly expect that an economics professor from Stanford would have a more informed view of the benefits and costs of socialized medicine than would a farmer in a small village in India. For people concerned with thoroughly understanding the issues of abortion, more information and more questioning of the advocates is essential—whether you are for, or against it.

The Platonic views of how Socrates searched for truth are crucial. Ask a question, then question the answer, then question that answer, then question that new answer. When examining opinions and definitions, as we do with value questions, like abortion or capital punishment or equality. These value questions can be clarified, questioned, and debated—but seldom, if ever, are settled. They are based on assumptions and are seldom subject to empirical verification—although often empirical evidence can be used to attempt to verify or criticize evidence offered to support a position taken by those who support one position or another.

The positions that people take on abortion, pro or con, have arguments that can be rationally understood. They are more subject to analysis than some of the Medieval theological arguments such as: how many angels can dance on the head of a pin? So we will flit back and for between science, philosophy, and religion in our attempt to understand the various arguments and to look deeper into them. Such analysis may upset some people who haven't thoroughly understood the opinions that they fiercely defend. But understanding the issues is the task of this treatise!

So, we had better start at the beginning. Sadly, many, who will not read this book, will start at the end. They start with an opinion, then look feverishly for ideas that will back up their opinion.

STAGES OF PREGNANCY

So, a major question is "at what point do we define life as existing?" Often this question is posed as, "when does personhood begin." Let us look at the stages of pregnancy to see the many points where people have said that life begins.

To get a clearer picture of what happens during pregnancy, most high level authorities (i.e., The American College of Obstetricians and Gynecologists) mark pregnancy as beginning at the date of the last menstrual cycle. Most doctors (57%) say that pregnancy starts at fertilization. So, when life begins and when pregnancy begins are really two different questions let's look at it week to week.

The American College of Obstetricians and Gynecologists' position is the timetable we will use.

Weeks 1 & 2. The ovum is released during this time.

Week 3. It will be fertilized in the fallopian tube (it is now called a zygote) and immediately begins dividing. It implants in about a week and the group of cells is now called a blastocyst. Further division makes it into what we call an embryo, then eventually a fetus. The blastocyst will probably implant into the wall of the uterus, about 10 days after fertilization. Some of these will never implant in the uterus and the woman will probably never realize that she had carried a fertilized ovum.

Sometimes a developing zygote or blastocyst splits during this period and identical twins result.

Week 5. The developing cells are now in the embryonic stage, so the growing cells are called an embryo. Here the cells begin to differentiate into specific organs such as: blood, kidneys, and nerves-- the brain and spinal column, as well as the heart, begin to differentiate from the original generalized cells. (This is the time that the embryo is most likely to be affected by infections, drug or alcohol use, certain medicines, etc.)

Weeks 6 & 7. Buds appear on the embryo which will become the arms and legs. The brain is beginning to develop, the heart beats, blood begins to move through the tissues, and the eyes and ears begin to develop.

Week 8. The lungs begin to form. The arms and legs continue to grow. The hands and feet are like little paddles,

Week 9. The hair follicles begin to form and the organs are beginning to grow.

Week 10. The ears begin to take shape, the facial features continue to form. At this point the embryo is now termed a fetus.

Weeks 11 to 14. The liver is making blood cells, the face is pretty well formed, the genitals begin to form. The head is about the size of the rest of its body.

Weeks 15 to 18. Muscles and bones continue to form, the liver and pancreas begin to produce secretions, the skin is somewhat transparent, the fetus now begins to stretch and move.

Weeks 19 to 21. The fetus can hear. It continues to be active.

Week 22. The hair and nails grow. There is more fetal activity. It may be able to survive outside the body.

Weeks 23 to 25. The bone marrow begins to make blood cells, the lower airways of the baby's lungs develop.

Week 26. The air sacs begin to develop in the lungs. The eyes are developed.

Weeks 27 to 30. The brain grows rapidly, eyelids can open and close. The lungs continue to develop.

Weeks 31 to 34. Fetus gains a great deal of fat; the lungs are not yet mature but breathing occurs. The bones are developed but are soft. The body begins storing iron, calcium, and phosphorus.

Weeks 35 to 37. The fetus weighs about 5 1/2 pounds. It develops sleeping patterns. The heart and blood vessels are complete.

Weeks 38 to 40. Breast nipples are seen in both sexes. Hair on the head appears course and thicker. The fetus now can be born at any time.

SO WHEN DOES LIFE START?

Does life start: when the ovum is released (the ovum is alive), when it is fertilized (the sperm was also alive), when it implants, when the heart starts beating, when brain waves start in the brain stem, when brain waves start in the cerebrum, when it is born—or sometime later. Whichever time you choose it is merely an opinion or a definition. Even if you have a democratic vote on it—it is merely an opinion.

Laws are often based on the opinions of the legislators. These opinions may, or may not, be true. For example, if Congress passed a law that the Earth was flat, so long distance air carriers could no longer fly the polar routes, this would be legal—it would not, however, be true. Similarly, defining when life starts and codifying it as a law is merely codifying a definition. As we will now indicate, there are many criteria that might be used in determining when life starts. However, it is only an opinion of a definition that is based on one or several factors.

As an illustration, when an atom was found to contain one proton and one electron and was called hydrogen, we had a definition. You might want to call it oxygen, but there is universal agreement to call it hydrogen. We have therefore defined hydrogen as an atom with one proton and one electron. Defining when life starts is not quite that simple, although there are people willing to kill or be killed to protect their definition. How we define life does not make our opinion true!

SO, WHEN DOES LIFE START?

BEFORE CONCEPTION

The Mormon belief, based on Abraham 3:23 (a scripture limited to the Mormon faith), is that the soul existed before the physical body was formed.

In 2012, the Arizona governor signed a bill that pinpoints the start of life two weeks before conception—corresponding to the American College of Obstetricians and Gynecologists position of when pregnancy begins. This had the effect of shortening the time during which one might opt for an abortion. It was struck down by the federal court.

Both the sperm and the ovum were alive before fertilization. In humans, non-living things cannot create living tissues. About 4 billion years ago, living cells evolved from non-living matter—but that doesn't happen in the human body.

AT CONCEPTION

The Catholic religion, since 1869, has had the belief that life starts at conception. Many Protestants also believe this—especially the evangelicals.

For "test tube" (in vitro) fertilizations, where the sperm and ovum are connected in a laboratory, we must assume that the soul is infused into that ovum in the laboratory before it is implanted into the woman's uterus. So the soul will be in the laboratory containers for 5 to 7 days, before it is implanted. But what if the test tube breaks? Does the soul go to that Great Laboratory in the Sky, or does it just fly around the lab waiting for another test tube containing zygote?

In 1859, the American Medical Association published a statement strongly opposing abortion, particularly commenting on the independence of the zygote during the time between its formation and its implantation.

AT IMPLANTATION

Although the American College of Obstetrics and Gynecology in 1965 attempted to redefine "conception" to mean implantation rather than fertilization, medical dictionaries and even English language dictionaries both before and after 1966, define "conception" as synonymous with fertilization.

DURING PREGNANCY

Prior to 1869 most Catholic thinking was that males got their souls 40 days after conception, about the time they were becoming fetuses and females got theirs 40 or 50 days later. Consequently, an abortion of a male fetus prior to that 40-day mark or a female prior to the 80-day mark might be acceptable. However, many Catholic theologians had always considered abortion to be immoral. (The term "conception" had been used since pre-Christian times, but it was not explained and proven until the late 1800s, so it was a meaningless concept before it was understood.)

On the other hand, embryos with developmental problems naturally miscarry, that is called a spontaneous abortion. For many who have strong God-based values, it can be explained as abortions caused by God. There are far more of these spontaneous abortions than human caused abortions.

WHEN BORN ALIVE

The Jewish view traditionally is that the child is a person when it is born and takes his first breath. However, there are rabbis who believe Aristotle's idea of ensoulment at 40 days, and others believe that it does not happen until the child can first say "Amen."

The United States Code, 1 para 8, as enacted in 2002 mentions "live birth" as the criterion for being human.

> "Person", "human being", "child", and "individual" as including born-alive infant
>
> (a) In determining the meaning of any Act of Congress, or of any ruling, regulation, or interpretation of the various administrative bureaus and agencies of the United States, the words "person", "human being", "child", and "individual", shall include every infant member of the species homo sapiens who is born alive at any stage of development.

(b) As used in this section, the term "born alive", with respect to a member of the species homo sapiens, means the complete expulsion or extraction from his or her mother of that member, at any stage of development, who after such expulsion or extraction breathes or has a beating heart, pulsation of the umbilical cord, or definite movement of voluntary muscles, regardless of whether the umbilical cord has been cut, and regardless of whether the expulsion or extraction occurs as a result of natural or induced labor, cesarean section, or induced abortion.

(c) Nothing in this section shall be construed to affirm, deny, expand, or contract any legal status or legal right applicable to any member of the species homo sapiens at any point prior to being "born alive" as defined in this section.

OTHER POSSIBILITIES FOR DETERMINING THE START OF LIFE

We might start with when does life end. If death occurs when the heart stops, then we should probably say that life starts when the heart starts.

If we use the idea of brain death as the criterion for dying then the brain waves' beginning would be the start of life. If we believe that death occurs when the brain waves in the cerebral cortex, where the higher human mental functions occur, cease to exist, then we would see life beginning around the 23rd week after conception. If we use the death of the total brain, including the brainstem, as the criterion for death, then the beginning of brain waves in the brainstem would be the beginning of life. This would occur around seven weeks after conception.

So, when does human life start?: At conception, at implantation, at ensoulment, when consciousness begins, or when reasoning ability begins-- as philosopher Immanuel Kant believed. There is certainly a continuum of beliefs, from conception to reasoning ability.

We will look at this in greater detail in later chapters.

We might ask whether a potential person has the same value as an existing person. In legal wrongful death cases, a father who is killed in an accident is worth much more money than his child who was killed in the same accident. The father was more valuable to his family, and to society.

WHAT ABOUT PERSONHOOD?

Personhood is the status that has the pro- and anti-abortion groups arguing. When does it occur? When life starts? When meaningful life starts? When pregnancy begins? When the soul enters the body? When the newborn is recognized as a potentially useful citizen? When the adult actually becomes a useful citizen?

The Stoics and the Jews believed that it happened when the baby took its first breath.

We may well have different definitions of "life" or "meaningful life" and therefore different points along the continuum of human development at which our personal definition fits. But we must recognize that it is only an opinion and a definition—even though it may be written into law, or accepted by a religion as a profound belief or dogma.

Becoming an individual separate from one's parents is a key factor. This individualization may be seen as occurring by different people at: fertilization, implantation, when it is a separate person or twin sometime within the first 14 to 20 days of existence, when the heart begins to beat, when the central nervous system matures, when the fetus can first feel pain, when it first shows movement, when it is able to recognize people.

The word "person," as used in the Fourteenth Amendment, does not include the unborn. This is in accord with the results reached in those few cases where the issue has been decided in courts.

ENSOULMENT

Even though it is not always mentioned in the arguments against abortion, the Western idea of soul is implied, and usually assumed, by the pro-life people. Most are pro-human life. Some are pro-any animal life. Some members of PETA (People for the Ethical Treatment of Animals) and Jains, an ancient Indian religion, whose followers do not eat meat, would be examples of people believing in a "soul" or "life force" that is similar in all of us "animals.".

Western monotheistic religions are likely to believe that human life, or even personhood, begins when the soul enters the body. If the zygote, embryo, or fetus is a "person," killing it would probably be called "murder." Throughout history, this "ensoulment" has been believed to happen at different times, such as: at conception, when the fetus has developed human features, or when it is born and takes its first breath. Religions of the East, like Hinduism, Shinto, or Buddhism have quite different views.

Each of us tends to believe what our parents told us—and what is commonly believed in our society. So, our opinions and definitions are developed locally. They are not universal opinions shared by all people. And, of course, many people do not believe that such a thing as a soul exists.

In the arguments for and against abortion, the critical questions are: whether or not a soul exists—and if it does, when does it enter the body. To study the question in an historical context, we must look at the appropriate religious scriptures and at the philosophical arguments that lend credence to them-- or question them. Since today's philosophers are more likely to be influenced by empirical science, that is facts or theories that are highly probable or "true," we must return to the early days of philosophy when what seemed reasonable was accepted. This was the time that it was obvious that the Earth was flat and that the sun revolved around the Earth.

Since "personhood" and "soul" are concepts that cannot be proven, we must look to pre-scientific "rational" thinkers—like the Golden Age philosophers of Greece. Some of the ancient Greek writers thought that "soul" was a life force that was totally extinguished on death. This would be the position of today's atheists. Other ancients thought that it was the entity which would live forever in the underworld. For those in the Western religions, it would be the entity that would live forever in Paradise or in Hell.

The word "soul" is generally used when translating the Greek term for the "life force" that causes growth in plants, sensation and movement in animals, and the ability to think rationally in humans. This is quite a different meaning than the current religious concept used in the West for the last 2000 years.

In a Western religious sense, "soul" is usually used to mean the essence or the image of God. In Genesis (1:26-27), it says, "So God created man in his own image." If we are to move a thousand or more years later, we find in the New Testament that God is spirit. (John 4:24) One might ask if we are being rational when we connect the first book of the Bible to the last of the gospel writers. There would be about 1300 years that had elapsed between the two authors. For those who believe that the Bible is "the inspired word of God," it is not a problem. For those who see the Bible as a collection of writings illustrating historical, ethical, and often conflicting ideas about the Supernatural and Jewish history, they might be skeptical of the connection.

This semantic change tends to confuse those who think deeply. Aristotle did not mean that the soul was the image of God. This was a Biblical idea. He thought of it as the essence that gives life, then eventually, the ability to reason. For him, there were evolving levels of this life force.

As Christianity developed, it looked more and more to the various philosophies of ancient Greece to clarify the meaning of the Bible. Aristotle was the most far-reaching thinker of the Golden Age of Greece. Plato, his teacher, was probably second. Some of the early church fathers used Plato, as did St. Augustine. More often, it was Aristotle who was the chosen model. Thomas Aquinas, the leading theologian of the Christian (Catholic) Church used Aristotle almost exclusively in his works summing up Christian theology.

The definitions of soul, meaning life force, used in the translations of Aristotle, contain three different meanings of this life force. Humans first become like plants in early pregnancy and have the vegetative soul that is merely the factor in growth, reproduction, and nutrition. Later, the life force develops as in animals, and is the factor influencing perception and movement. The human life force develops about the time of movement of the fetus. This would be about 40 days after conception for males and 80 to 90 days after conception for females. This would be the "soul" that senses things. The last stage of soul, according to Aristotle, was the development of the ability to reason. Only humans have this. Christian thinkers, like Aquinas, felt that this was the "image of God" that the Bible had mentioned.

We will look at the writings of Aristotle for a few minutes. Aristotle's ideas were

15

fundamental to Christian (Catholic) ideas from the Middle Ages. His thinking became very important in the Middle Ages with both Christian and Muslim thinkers. Towards the end of the Middle Ages, some Islamic writers downplayed the influence of Aristotle because his rationalism (using the power of human reasoning to direct one's life) might result in a loss of faith.

In the mid-13th century, Thomas Aquinas, the leading Christian (Catholic) thinker, Christianized Aristotle. In his books, Summa Theologica, He continued the reasoning of Aristotle while applying it to Biblical teaching.

When the soul enters the body is a major question for some religions. The ideas in the Western religions generally begin with the writings of Aristotle from a few centuries before Jesus. He wrote, as we mentioned, that male babies received their souls about 40 days after conception, while females received theirs about 50 days later. He believed that females were inferior to males.

Pope Gregory XIV, in 1590, eased the prior papal decrees that would excommunicate any woman who had an abortion at any time, changing it to abortion only after the fetus was formed. In fact, aborting a female fetus prior to the 80th day of pregnancy could be acceptable as long as there was no soul yet infused. Others thought that because a fetus in the uterus does not have the ability to reason, that is, it does not have a rational soul, abortion could be possible. But Pope Pius IX in 1869, removed all doubt about when the soul was infused. It was at conception.

Muslim thinking on ensoulment has ranged from the soul being infused at any time from 40 to 120 days. The Sunni belief is generally that no abortion should be allowed at any time.

Looking at the Hindu idea of the supernatural, all of the universe is God. Consequently, nothing can be created or destroyed.

SO, LET'S LOOK A BIT DEEPER AT THE ASSUMPTIONS AND FACTS THAT CONFUSE US ON THIS QUESTION

In any controversial question, there are at least two sides to the story. People's views on abortion often stem from their traditions. They might be religious. They might be financial. They might be the needs of a society. Thinking will start with a non-provable basic assumption as to which entity is primary—

> Oneself,

> What one believes that his or her God wants,

> What is best for one's ideas of what an ideal society should be.

Once that basic assumption is determined, empirical facts, strong opinions, and plausible theories must be brought into focus. We will still have disagreements because basic assumptions cannot be proven-- and facts, no matter how probable, will be countered with strong opinions. Which do I believe?

➢	What I think the Bible says, or

➢	The proven, or incredibly probable, theories of Darwin or Einstein.

With these thoughts in mind, let us look at the issue of abortion and how it may affect our societies—both pro and con.

All of the arguments about abortion, and most other value choices, deal with both values and the wider field of ethics. In the following chapters, we will look much deeper into the general area of ethics and the specific values choices that are possible with the issue of abortion. The two traditional positions—a woman's right to choose and the religious idea that abortion is murder—are only two possibilities. And, they may not be the most important reasons that might be given.

As mentioned, our values come from three sources: self-centered values, what we believe are God based values, and what we believe are values for the best society. Obviously, in arguments used in the above paragraph, those women who wanted an abortion were in the self-centered value area, and those who were against abortion were in the God-based area.

In the Roe versus Wade case, the Supreme Court ruled for the self-centered desires as being primary for freedom. As you can see, making a better society has not been a reason for abortion in the US. However, some significant research indicates that the drop in crime 20 years after the Roe decision was the result of unwanted babies not being born.

Abortion was considered a social necessity in China 40 years ago. By adopting the "one child policy" and requiring abortions of additional pregnancies, the Chinese government reduced its population explosion. 400,000,000 fewer babies were born in China during the years of the one child policy. This allowed more money for the expansion of business and trade and more money for education. Some of the Chinese universities are now among the best in the world.

These basic reasons for choosing our values are considered to be "basic assumptions." "Basic" because they are at the rock-bottom level of our thinking on an issue, and "assumptions," because they cannot really be proven to be true. We can't empirically prove that a creating and all-knowing being exists. We can't prove what type of society is best. Some philosophers of the past even doubted that we existed as bodies—they thought that we are merely ideas in the mind of God. But I assume that you will agree with me-- that we do exist as real bodies!

SELF-CENTERED ASSUMPTIONS.

We certainly assume that we exist, and there is good reason for it. In philosophy, this would be a belief in materialism or realism. Real objects exist. But there are some, including very important philosophers, usually in the past, who believed that ideas were the primary stuff of the universe. Bishop Berkeley, an Anglican bishop and one of the greatest thinkers of the past, made a very strong case for everything being idea. Of course, God would be the major idea. In fact, he made the case that we do not exist, we are all ideas in the mind of God. So, if philosophers like Berkeley are right, we can question the first basic assumption, that our desires are worthy of consideration. But I suggest that we forget thinkers like Berkeley and assume that our desires come from real people— like you and me.

GOD BASED ASSUMPTIONS.

While a great many people believe in some sort of a supernatural being, the characteristics of that being very considerably. And even when there are similarities in what that being is like, there are huge disagreements. There are several ideas of what that being is like. Today, the Christians, Muslims, Jews, and Baha'is believe in a theistic God. This God created the world and is involved in the world. It may or may not answer prayers. But it is, or should I say He is, the ultimate lawgiver and the all-powerful and all-knowing being that provides for heaven and hell in the afterlife.

A second type of God idea is the deistic being. This God created the world but is not concerned with what goes on in the world. So people who would believe in this type of God would not use God-based values or God-based assumptions. It was this type of being that many of the Founding Fathers subscribed to, like: Thomas Jefferson, George Washington, and Benjamin Franklin. There is no afterlife.

Another concept of a supernatural is the pantheistic god—the whole universe is god. The Hindu and related religions believe in this. The afterlife may be a series of reincarnations—and eventually when the person has lived a perfect life his essence will become an indistinguishable piece of the pantheistic whole.

Then there are the older, and often primitive beliefs, in polytheism. A god for the hunt, another for fertility, another for rain, and another for war. So, their beliefs were polytheistic. The afterlife can be in any number of pleasant environs, like a happy hunting ground.

The God based assumptions are much more complicated than the self-centered assumptions because there are so many ideas of supernaturals—and their varying powers and whims. Different religions have varying ideas of what the primary god or gods have done, what they require, and what their penchants for justice, mercy, or retribution may be.

If the God of the Aztecs required a number of young people to be thrown off of a cliff, that may be different from the idea of mercy that Jesus sometimes advocated. Some gods require sacrifices to appease them. We find this in many religions. Many religions also have the same golden rule of ethics, "do unto others as you would have them do unto you." Perhaps Christians would be moved by the words of Paul in his letter to the Romans (13:10) "Love worketh no ill to his neighbour: therefore love [is] the fulfilling of the law."

With so many ideas of a supernatural, or supernaturals, and with each society finding varying interpretations of the commands of their god or gods we can expect quite different opinions on values. For example, some religions are against abortion-- like the Catholics or Mormons. Some religions are noncommittal about abortion, like the Presbyterians and Unitarians-- who believe that is up to the pregnant person to decide.

In this book, when discussing God-based assumptions, we will emphasize the God-based assumptions and scriptures of the monotheistic religions because they are the primary beliefs of Western readers.

SOCIETY-BASED ASSUMPTIONS

Basing a decision on a version of society that one thinks is ideal, is a societal assumption. Like the God based assumptions, societal assumptions can vary greatly.

China has developed strong societal values, from the top down. Their "one child policy" was criticized by its populace and by governments and human rights groups around the world. What was the result? 400,000,000 fewer babies were born. This allowed more money for education, more money to develop its economic system, a huge reduction of poverty, and a number of other advantages to their society. Now that the ban has been lifted to allow for two children, most families prefer to have only one child.

Now we find that they have some of the top universities in the world. Their economy is now approaching number one in the world. With their per capita GDP at $16,500 they are only 76th in the world. The U.S. is 11th at $56,500. But their economy is now growing 3 times faster than that of the U.S. In the seven-year period starting in 2007 their purchasing power per person grew 61%, while the American consumer's purchasing power grew by only 11%.

Now China is installing many thousands of cameras daily to keep track of its people. Along with this, the government has developed a "social credit" system to reward people for living correctly, including paying their taxes. The good citizens will be rewarded by preferential treatment, such as buying travel tickets. Do the plusses of an orderly and progressing society outweigh the personal freedoms and rights to privacy that are somewhat more available in the West? This is the question of self-interest versus the interests of a society.

Applying societal needs to the question of abortion--if the society to which one attaches himself or herself needs more soldiers or consumers--abortion might possibly be made illegal in that society. But if the society already has too many people, like China, India and most Mideast, African, and South American countries-- abortion might be made mandatory.

THE ASSUMPTIONS WE USE MAY VARY WITH THE VALUE WE ARE CONSIDERING

We all may hold each of these three different assumptions depending on the issue. Perhaps, when it is cold, I want to wear my mink coat-- even though many people believe that raising animals for their skins is immoral. I would be using a self-centered value. I may be a Catholic, so I am against abortion. This is obviously a God basis. At the same time, I may be working for the Green Party to reduce carbon dioxide pollution. This would be a society-based value. But it could also be a God-based value. Looking at a few verses from Genesis we can see some "God assumptions" implied:

1:26 "And God said, Let us make man in our image, after our likeness: and let them have dominion over the fish of the sea, and over the fowl of the air, and over the cattle, and over all the earth, and over every creeping thing that creepeth upon the earth."

1:28 "And God blessed them, and God said unto them, Be fruitful, and multiply, and replenish the earth, and subdue it: and have dominion over the fish of the sea, and over the fowl of the air, and over every living thing that moveth upon the earth."

If God gave dominion "over all the earth," and commanded us to "subdue" the earth, we could certainly make a case for a God basis here. But Genesis does not specifically mention climate change.

LET'S LOOK AT ANOTHER VALUE QUESTION IN AMERICAN SOCIETY

Before examining abortion arguments in detail, let us look briefly at what may be America's major health problem-- the opioid addiction levels. What if we have a person we do not know who is a fentanyl addict, and has been for five years. He has been in treatment centers three times, but does not want to give up his habit because it feels so good. Should we just let him die on his next overdose?

His sister and mother want to protect him and hope he will give up his habit. Their desires are self-centered.

We have some people in the Salvation Army who have taken him into their shelters and fed him. Since all people are created in the image of God, all of us are equally valuable and the Salvation Army follows this ethical idea.

On the other hand, there are people who believe that anyone who chooses to use addicting drugs is not worthy of the society. Why should our society spend police time, ambulance driver time, doctor and nurse time, on this derelict? We would be better off spending the money on schools and scholarships for people who have a good chance of helping society. After all, there is only so much money for society to use. So, where are the best places to put our tax dollars for the betterment of our society?

NOW BACK TO ABORTION

As we have emphasized, nearly every ethical issue comes down to where we stand on our particular assumption-- whether it be self, God, or society. Here is a brief illustration of how the three types of value assumptions may be used, both pro and con, in the abortion question. Later in this treatise, we will introduce other arguments and go deeper into the underlying foundations of each of these positions-- many of which are not understood or not thought deeply about by the people who espouse the argument.

SELF-CENTERED REASONS FOR WANTING AN ABORTION

"I am pregnant and I don't want to have a child." This is probably the overriding reason for people wanting the freedom of choice. As with Roe versus Wade, this freedom was seen as a right to privacy under Point V of the decision. So, what weight do we put on the desires of an individual in a society in which freedom is a primary constitutional value?

SELF-CENTERED REASONS FOR NOT WANTING AN ABORTION

What if I don't want the child, but my boyfriend wants it. Or what if my mother wants a grandchild? For them, my abortion would not have value for them. So, some countries and religions require the husband's permission for an abortion. So, if he wants the child, the abortion would be immoral and illegal.

GOD BASED REASONS FOR WANTING AN ABORTION

You are pregnant and want the child, but you are a drug addict who has never shown any ability to love or be empathetic. My God-based reasoning might to be that the child will likely be mistreated severely and will have little hope of leading a life that will get him to heaven. Another God reason for advocating abortions would be that the mother is either nonreligious or in a different religion that is not likely to raise a person who can enter Paradise. It is unmerciful to bring people into the world who do not have an excellent chance of going to heaven.

GOD-BASED REASONS FOR NOT WANTING ABORTIONS

The major reason for always preventing abortions came from Pope Pius IX in 1869. It was only then that a religion determined that meaningful life began at conception. It was at this moment that the soul was implanted into the fertilized ovum.

We might wonder about the Biblical ideas about abortion, which is not specifically mentioned, and wonder if we should advocate practices that are mentioned-- such as slavery.

In Exodus 21:20 it states that: "Anyone who beats their male or female slave with a rod must be punished if the slave dies as a direct result; 21:21 but they are not to be punished if the slave recovers after a day or two, since the slave is their property.

And two verses later it says that, "If people are fighting and hit a pregnant woman and she gives birth prematurely but there is no serious injury, the offender must be fined whatever the woman's husband demands and the court allows. But if there is serious injury, you are to take life for life, eye for eye, tooth for tooth, hand for hand, foot for foot, burn for burn, wound for wound, bruise for bruise." This section obviously demands capital punishment in certain cases, and even what some people might call, "cruel and unusual punishment."

At verse 26 it again approves of slavery generally, saying, "An owner who hits a male or female slave in the eye and destroys it must let the slave go free to compensate for the eye. And an owner who knocks out the tooth of a male or female slave must let the slave go free to compensate for the tooth."

Some have asked whether those strong in the God-based ethical areas of the Bible, might be more consistent in their values if they followed the Scriptures of their religions more closely.

SOCIETAL REASONS FOR WANTING ABORTIONS LEGAL

When a society has too many people, as China determined in 1980, abortion may be allowed or even required to control the population. In today's world, with climate change threatening the world society, societies might require, or recommend, abortions to control global warming. It is after all, the people who are causing this warming. Whether it is the open fires of primitive tribes cooking, or the fossil fuel use among the more advanced societies, too many people is the cause of the problem.

Another major reason for having abortions legal is that every child, wanted or unwanted, costs the society higher taxes for education. For example, in the United States, the current cost of educating a child through high school is about $120,000. It is strange that quite often people who are against abortion for religious reasons are also for lower taxes for self-centered reasons. This is just one of the many areas in which our values may conflict.

Another reason for allowing for abortions occurs if the freedom of the citizens is a major factor in the precepts of the society. In the American government, liberty is the major factor spelled out in the Bill of Rights. Amendment 9 states that, " The enumeration in the Constitution of certain rights shall not be construed to deny or disparage others retained by the people." And the 10th Amendment states that, "The powers not delegated to the United States by the Constitution, nor prohibited by it to the states, are reserved to the states respectively, or to the people."

The Ninth Amendment seems to give more power to the people. The 10th amendment is not as clear, in that certain powers can be reserved by the states or by the people. Using this logic, states could forbid abortion. Or the power could be retained by the people. This might indicate that a referendum might be required for the people to overrule a law developed by their representatives in the state government.

When a society needs more workers, soldiers, or consumers, it may want many more children, even if the parents do not want them. Russia today is in great need of more workers. The present-day workers have protested vehemently against President Putin's proposals to increase the age for retirement. Soon there will only be two workers per retiree. Japan has similar problems, in that they have the oldest population in the world. Possibly because of this Japan, is more restrictive than many countries in allowing abortions. Russia, once the pioneer in "abortion on demand," is now attempting to curb this freedom with minor changes in the laws. Still Russia leads the world in abortions.

MORE CONFLICTS IN VALUES

Often our values are thwarted. When the Supreme Court sided with the self-centered value of wanting an abortion and the society value of individual freedom, those God-based people who believed that abortion was murder were highly frustrated. They have worked hard to have anti-abortion legislators, executives, and judges elected. As states passed legislation making abortions harder to obtain-- it was the people. who wanted the freedom of the individual to make her own choices about her body. who were frustrated.

But often, as individuals, we have conflicts in our values. A major conflict is often found in individuals who consider themselves to be conservative. For example, many of the people who oppose abortion, want lower taxes. Since every child, wanted or unwanted, is required to go to school. As we have mentioned, if the unwanted child goes to a public school, the average cost of educating him or her through high school is about $120,000. If the child is poor, tax-paid Medicaid will add to the expenses of the Federal and the state governments. If that child runs afoul of the law, as many unwanted and unloved young ones do-- police, judicial, and penal expenses must be paid by the taxpayer. The average cost of imprisoning a juvenile is $120,000 per year. If he or she commits a serious crime that requires life imprisonment, the cost could exceeed one million dollars.

Another conflict might occur to a person who held the societal value of fighting climate change and was against abortion. But every child, wanted or unwanted, adds about 6,000 tons of carbon dioxide and other greenhouse gasses to the atmosphere in a lifetime. But it doesn't end there! Their progeny continue to add such gasses until the last descendant has died.

A conflict that affects American citizens is the recent international question of conflicts of values arose when President Trump canceled the wargames of South Korea and the US as a gesture of goodwill towards North Korea. The societal interests of North Korea were served, but South Korea's interests, according them, were not served. So we have a conflict in societal values.

President Trump said that the games cost Americans hundreds of millions of dollars. The actual cost, according to the Pentagon, was $14 million. All of the service people are already on salary. The only expense was to bring them to South Korea from Guam and neighboring islands. So here we have a conflict between what the president says about saving money, in order to back up his position, versus what the American citizens need to know.

Another conflict in values is that if saving money for the American society is important, Trump's golfing expeditions cost far more than Korean-American wargames. In his first 20 months of his presidency, he played golf 154 times. Many of these were at this hotel in Florida. The estimates from the General Accounting Office are that it costs $3.6 million per trip. (This includes $180,000 per hour for Air Force One; plus the cost of other planes to carry administrative and security staff; the movement, accommodations and food of essential security and administrative personnel; the rental of golf carts from his hotel for the secret service, etc.) The low estimate of costs for one year are $13.6 million by NBC to $90 million for his first 26 months by another group. We can assume that the ten trips a year to Mira-Lago cost about $36 million—about 250% of the South Korean war games.

So what Trump said is an important savings for the nation in one instance. A societal value, is more than countered by his self-centered interest in his recreation and income for his hotel.

These conflicts are present in most value areas and with most people. A person may want a congenial democratic society that enjoys free speech, but protest when one of opposite views is given a "soap box." This has happened often recently, when conservatives have been invited to speak at college campuses.

SOME MORE STATISTICS

8.6% of abortions reported to the Centers for Disease Control and Prevention in 2014 were undergone by women who had three or more previous abortions; 45% of abortions were undergone by women who had one or more previous abortions.

While only a little more than a third of the American abortions are performed on blacks, since about 12% of Americans are African Americans, it would give an abortion rate of nearly three times that of the whites. However, since 75% of Americans are Caucasian and half of abortions are to whites, this also raises the percentage of abortions for whites.

Since the Roe v. Wade Supreme Court decision in 1973 there have been about 50 million abortions in the U.S. About 30% of women have had them. The reasons given are:

> 25% not ready for another child/timing is wrong

24

- ➤ 23% can't afford a baby now
- ➤ 19% have completed childbearing/have other people depending on me/children are grown
- ➤ 8% don't want to be a single mother/or are having relationship problems
- ➤ 7% don't feel mature enough to raise a(nother) child or they feel that they are too young
- ➤ 4% would interfere with education or career plans
- ➤ 4% physical problem with their health
- ➤ 3% possible problems affecting the health of the fetus
- ➤ 0.5% husband or partner wants me to have an abortion
- ➤ 0.5% parents want me to have an abortion
- ➤ 0.5% don't want people to know I had sex or got pregnant
- ➤ 0.5% was a victim of rape

To the above list, we might add:

- ➤ Being pregnant from an incestual encounter
- ➤ A risk for the life or health (mental or physical) of the mother
- ➤ Serious fetal problem

So, this lays out some of the issues we will discuss in more detail in Chapters 4, 5, and 6. But first we need to look at the general theory of ethics-- of what is right.

CHAPTER 2 A BRIEF LOOK AT ETHICS

Ethics deal with what is right. But determining what is right is not that simple! Should it be based only on what I want for me? Is it moral if I want to commit suicide? Will my mother see my suicide as having value for her? Or, I am very poor and very pregnant. I want a child but can't support it. Should I have an abortion?

Thinking deeply into our beliefs or opinions requires us to delve into the areas that the field of philosophy has investigated for millennia. This is not a book on philosophy, but whenever people discuss an issue in detail, they will be in the area of philosophy—whether they know ir or not.

> Most of our discussion in this treatise is about WHY you believe something. Are your beliefs based on assumptions that are self-centered, God-based, or society based? These are areas that are starting points of thinking that go beyond (*meta*) our physical world. This is the area called *metaphysics*.

> How we "know" is in the area of philosophy called epistemology. (*Episteme* is the Greek word for knowledge.)

> To what degree are our ideas empirically provable or highly probable? This is in the area of science and inductive logic.

> Are your intentions or actions "right?" This is the area of ethics.

We will use this chapter to look at this fourth area of concern since we will refer back to it in the next chapters, where we discuss the first two areas of our thinking about values.

ETHICAL PRECEPTS

Ethics, depending on the speaker, can depend on what is fair, what gives the greatest amount of happiness, what one thinks that God wants, or what will deliver the desired society the quickest. It might also use one's intention or the actual consequences of the action. Let's look at some criteria for what is ethical.

WHAT IS FAIR

Immanuel Kant's classical ethical precept is **that you should never use people as a means**

to your own end or desires, but always see people as ends in themselves. Laissez-faire capitalism would be an example of the unethical approach where any means of advertising or promotion would make me money, even if the buyer were cheated. The capitalist warning that "let the buyer beware," is an indication that the buyer may be fooled, and if so, it is his or her fault.

The recent election of Donald Trump in America, and the British referendum to leave the European Union are prime examples of violations of Kant's dictum. In both cases people were lied to repeatedly. Two major examples:

In the Brexit referendum, a major lie was that by leaving the EU hundreds of millions of dollars (350 million pounds) a week could be saved and used by the National Health Service. The day after the vote it was admitted that it was a lie. The number was 120 million pounds and it would not go to the NHS.

The major Trump promise was that he would build a wall on the southern border of the U.S. and that Mexico would pay for it. The realities were that:

> Much of the area to be used for the wall was owned by citizens or Indian tribes who did not want the wall, so eminent domain cases to take their land might take years to settle;

> The wall would not affect the many tunnels that now exist, or could be built in the future; Mexico was adamant that it would never pay for the wall; and,

> The cost to the U.S. taxpayer, who was already paying more to the government because of the higher consumer costs required to pay for the Trump-imposed tariffs;

> If other funds were used to build the wall, existing government program would have to be cut, or, if the Congress voted for an increase in the national debt to fund it, each citizen would be even more indebted, since each already owes about $65,000 on the existing national debt and that amount has now been increased by $3,600 to pay for the $1.2 trillion cost of his tax cuts for corporations, and the rich individuals.

The manipulation of social media by the winning parties, and the manipulation of the media by outside forces (like Russia) may have been critical to the outcomes.

In America, in Nazi Germany, and in most Mid-East, African, and South American countries, and many others, Kant's rule is honored only in its breach.

Kant's idea can be seen to have implications for all three basic assumptions. From a self-centered point of view, we might have an implied contract that "I will not treat you as a means to my end, if you don't treat me as a means to your ends." It could also be used from a religious point of view, particularly the Judeo-Christian idea that we are all made in the image of God. We should not, therefore, be used as means to someone else's ends since we are of ultimate value. From a societal basis, it could be seen as a fundamental aspect of a social contract-- how we should treat each other.

Most religions have a golden rule that states, "Do unto others as you would have them do unto you." In some religions, it is stated as a negative. "Do not do to someone else that which you would not like done to yourself." These ethical rules, while commonly coming from religions, could just as easily be derived from a society-based ethic. In fact, it could also be derived from a self-centered value. "If you don't steal from me, I won't steal from you."

We can see that this idea of fairness is based on the idea that people are equal.

HAPPINESS

Some ancient and modern ethical systems begin with the individual, and what will bring happiness to that person. Some say, "eat, drink, and be merry-- for tomorrow we die." Others, still concerned with the individual, see higher levels of pleasure that should be pursued. So, Beethoven rather than beer, Plato rather than pasta, Dostoevsky rather than dancing the night away, and friendships rather than fornication. So there may be varying qualities of good that we might consider.

Jeremy Bentham developed the idea of utilitarianism. He believed that the most ethical concern was to have the greatest good for the greatest number of people.

Here we can also see that equality is important. Every person counts as one.

The idea of promoting "the greatest good, for the greatest number," is, of course, a societally based ethical precept. Democracy is based on this kind of thinking. However, what if a person's individual rights are violated in giving the majority the happiness that they desire? Should it be ethical to be prejudiced against all Jews, all Catholics, all Muslims, all the mentally ill? This would definitely violate the fairness principle expressed by Kant. Similarly, if the majority voted to tax high income earners to fund the needs or desires of the voting majority, that rich person may be seen as being a means to the ends of the majority. So, the ethical precepts that are most commonly used may at times be conflicting.

If we are to vote on pleasures that we want, such as: voting to give ourselves a new car, paid by the billionaire citizens; or voting for the right to see pornography, in opposition to what the religious citizens desire—be ethical? But we must be aware that pleasure is often different from happiness—so maybe seeking pleasure is ethically acceptable—if you follow some of Bentham's interpreters.

John Stuart Mill looked at Jeremy Bentham's ethical precept and decided that there are qualities of experiences that are of a higher-order then mere pleasure seeking, they can give a higher quality of happiness.

If the goal of ethical living should be maximizing one's happiness, any actions that reduce happiness are therefore immoral, while actions that increase happiness are moral and ethical.

However, there is disagreement over whether any pleasure is preferable to higher-level pleasures. Self-development, intellectual pleasures, like philosophy and art; or expressing the highest levels of character-- would be preferable to animal like pleasures. Similarly, the public good is superior to selfish goals.

THE WILL OF THE SUPERIOR PERSON SHOULD BE PRIMARY

Society might also be directed by the will of an exceptional person. The "great man theory of history" or the Nietzschean concept of the "overmen," might be viewed as being that--what the great men wanted was good for society—and was therefore the most ethical. In Nietzsche's case, the overmen were the only truly "human" people, the rest of us are just other animals, so should not be an ethical concern for the overmen. The overman's concern for you is similar to the superiority you probably feel over other animals How much are you concerned for the fate of the cow in your Big Mac?

We see something of this "values imposed from the top down" in modern China, where the elites of the Communist Party decide what is best for the country. The "one child policy," the channeling of the best potential academically or athletically gifted children into the appropriate areas where they can be successful and can contribute to the Chinese society are such examples. While freedom of speech and freedom of assembly have been put on the back burner of the Chinese stove, the economy of the country, the surge of world-class education, and its scientific achievements have dazzled the world.

WHAT DO THESE IDEAS HAVE TO DO WITH ABORTION?

So, what about abortion? From Kant's dictum, we can surmise that an individual should have the freedom to do as she wishes as long as she does not treat another person as a means to her end. Making a law or an ethical assertion that would force a person to become a means to someone else's desires, would be unethical. Of course, we could take the position of the embryo (assuming that it is a person) then, if the embryo wants to live, it would be unethical to abort it.

Being a "person" is a definition that cannot be empirically proven. As we have mentioned, some would say that personhood starts at conception. Others would say it starts at implantation. Others would say it would be when the heart started to beat or the brain waves were evident. Others would say it occurred at birth. Others would put personhood sometime after birth—like the ancient Spartans and other such groups. In Row v Wade, the Court rejected Texas's definition of life starting at conception.

There are people who seem to be willing to die for any one of their non-provable definitions. So making an ethical standard regarding abortion that could be applied to all situations and be agreed on by all people is not possible. There are too many opinions, based on the three basic assumptions, to have any chance of agreement. This also applies to most other value decisions-- capital punishment, torture, legalizing psychoactive drugs, are only a few of the value decisions in which the three assumptions are often in disagreement.

From Bentham's point of view, since it is a societally based assumption, abortion could be on-demand or prohibited, depending on the needs of the society. If the society needs more people, abortion could be made illegal-- or at least the exceptions to the law might be stringent, such as allowing for abortion in the cases of rape, incest, the health of the mother, or potential or actual infirmities of the fetus discovered in utero.

Values and ethics are not identical concepts. Values are in gradients from not being very important all the way up to an ethical precept. For example, if I have a question in my mind of the value of wearing a red sweater or a blue sweater today, this is a low level of value choice. If my question is whether or not to rob a bank, this question rates much higher in the value area. In fact, this becomes an ethical question because it is so high in the value hierarchy and it affects other people.

Ethical behavior usually is measured against how it affects other people. But it may not directly involve other people. Watching pornography involving non-consenting children may be unethical because of the use of the children as means to the ends of psychologically immature adults. But what if the people in the pornographic video were consenting adults, and perhaps paid for their performance? Here the performers were not being abused. Whether or not the viewing of the video was conducive to the mental health of the viewer could be an ethical consideration. Certainly, the viewer wanted to see the performance.

WHAT DO SOME SMART PEOPLE SAY?

Socrates, certainly one of the great minds our race has produced, said that a person must know all of the facts and the context from which they arise. Mere opinions are not enough. Opinions may only be wishes--either realistic or unrealistic, and may, or may not be, possible or probable.

While not having a knowledge of modern psychology, Socrates believed that people will do what is right, if they have sufficient knowledge. If we are all rational beings, he was right. But now we know that unconscious needs and drives commonly overcome rationality—and our modern reality often complicates the real issues with hacking, electronic propaganda, and the prominent platforms accorded to highly paid radio and television pundits. They continually distort the truth with no concern for logic. Their only concern is the size of their audiences—and their paycheckSo y!

Ancient thinkers commonly named happiness as the goal of life—and of ethics. But some equated happiness with the pleasures of the body, while others saw it as the pleasures of the mind.

Hedonism is the general term for the value of "maximizing pleasure while minimizing pain." This concept is a fundamental of the self-centered values mentioned earlier. Some men and women indulge in sex solely for the physical pleasure—that's hedonistic. But if pregnancy occurs, neither may want the pain of parenthood. That's hedonistic too. But many women want to keep their child conceived in pleasure. That's hedonistic too!

An extreme form of hedonism was espoused by Aristippus of Cyrene, who advocated for the immediate gratification of any pleasure. The future was not important, because that opportunity for pleasure might not present itself again. We saw this relatively recently in the beatniks of the 50s and the hippies of the 60s—where drugs and sex were primary concerns. Abortion, here, was certainly seen as having value.

Epicurus believed in pleasure, too, but like John Stuart Mill two millennia later, believed that some pleasures were detrimental to our real happiness. Overeating may lead to gastric unpleasantness. Overdrinking can lead to hangovers—and maybe alcoholism, and pleasurable sex may result in a sexually transmitted disease or an unwanted pregnancy—and the psychological and financial expense of an abortion.

Now let us look at how the varying values are developed, primarily in the question of abortion. We may stray occasionally from the major questions of this essay just to illustrate another major point of values.

INTENTION OR CONSEQUENCES—WHICH DETERMINES THE "RIGHTNESS" OF THE ACTION?

If you are driving your severely ill friend to the hospital and have an accident in which she was killed, was this a good action, or a bad one?

You are a Catholic with four children. Your husband is out of work and the bills are piling up. You have sex, using the Church's approved rhythm method, but you get pregnant. Should you bring another child into your impoverished family? So you have an abortion. Your intention was to save your future child from a potentially difficult life, but now you have severe guilt feelings. Was this decision ethical or unethical based on:

>   Your intention,

>   Your severe depression,

>   Your violation of your church's laws,

>   Because you saved the society money since it would not have to

educate the child, or provide other welfare benefits for it,

> That the child would have left a "carbon footprint" on the planet and contributed to global warming and climate change?

You had enjoyable sex, but now you are unhappily pregnant. My guess is that it wasn't worth it—so a bad value choice.

BASIC ASSUMPTIONS

Ethics, just as any organized body of thinking, rests on basic assumptions that we cannot prove. While they are basic to our argument, as we mentioned-- they cannot be proven. In fact, they are often such strong assumptions, they are usually considered to be true—without any doubt. I am reminded of a discussion I almost had with a Norwegian philosopher about why he believed that we are all equal. He would not discuss the possibility that our belief in equality rests on assumptions. Since examining the assumptions behind the concept of why people might believe in equality was the subject of my doctoral dissertation, I believed that philosophers should be able to discuss the subject! But no, he assumed the truth of his belief—so it was not open for discussion.

The same is true about discussing whether or not God exists. The late Steven Hawking, one of the great minds of civilization, in his final book, wrote that there is no creator of the universe. Would this convince any theists to change their long-held beliefs, that the Bible is the only source of truth in the world--and that it is the word of God? Highly unlikely!

Hawking's basic assumptions for his life's work dealt with the scientific method. It dealt with developing theories that would explain the realities that have been observed through telescopes and microscopes. The theist, on the other hand, believes in the statements of a book that his parents told him was true. If he is inquisitive, he spends his time attempting to verify the statements in the book. Some will even go as far as to search for Noah's Ark or the Garden of Eden.

We might be reminded that even modern science is based on certain assumptions. Many years ago Edwin Burtt, a devout theist, wrote a book, based on his doctoral dissertation. (The Metaphysical Foundations of Modern Science). While he criticized science, it does remind us that even science is based on assumptions. Among them are that:

> The natural world is responsible for all causes and effects;

> These is evidence in the natural world to explain all causes and effects;

> The exact same cause will have the exact same effect;

> As analytical tools (such as microscopes and telescopes) are developed, more answers to the questions of nature can be answered;

> The fewer the variables, the greater the probability of the conclusion;

> If an experiment is valid (actually measuring what it purports to measure), it

should be considered probable;

> If a probable theory is tested and retested, and the same results are obtained, it is a reliable probability;

The scientist attempts to find better sources of information and develop a more probable concept of the truth of an idea. Among the millions of questions that the various sciences seek answers to may be:

> How cancer develops in the pancreas and how it might be best treated;

> How the Earth's temperature is rising and why; and,

> What can be done to reverse the process; or,

> How the universe developed and what is the process of evolution?

The person who starts with an opinion then tries to prove that idea as true, is not really using the scientific method. They may try to prove that the meridians of acupuncture are involved in the curing of diseases. They may try to prove that Marx's theory of the eventuality of communism is inevitable. Or most commonly, they try to prove the realities of a religion, or a God, that were revealed to, or conjured up by, a person.

Many people use only one ethical criterion: the self, their God, or their society-- or of an ideal society. Most of us jump from one to another value basis depending on the issue. So I may want to smoke a joint of marijuana, read the Bible regularly every night, and work for the Communist Party in my leisure time. Here we have all three of the basic assumptions used in a short period of time.

We might also work to eliminate global warming while taking long automobile trips on the weekends. We are certainly familiar with the extensive sexual abuse of young people by Catholic priests. Here the self-centered desire for either power or sexual relief ran absolutely contrary to the vows of chastity that they took when entering the priesthood.

The two most commonly mentioned bases for ethics are those mentioned by Immanuel Kant and Jeremy Bentham. Do you subscribe to:

Treating everyone as an independent and valuable person and never using a person to fulfill your own needs and desires?

OR--

Running society for the greatest good for the greatest number?

Or are other ethical pronouncements primary? If you follow the scriptures of your religion, do you follow all of the commands and approved customs—or do you merely pick and choose?

If we are thinking people, we must know what and why we believe. If we are merely rocks, we can let the world go on around us and be unmoved.

CHAPTER 3 CONFLICTING DEFINITIONS AFFECTING OUR ARGUMENTATION

But before we proceed, we have some semantic problems we must be aware of--definitions of life, of human life, of murder, of God. These enter every argument. What is a clear-cut obvious definition for one person is often irrational, or at least non-provable, to another.

When people talk about killing unborn children in the first few weeks of pregnancy, should we use instead the biological and medical definitions in which we move from the single cell fertilized ovum called a zygote, which might be the thing aborted when using the 'morning after' pill. Is this an unborn child? It does have all the DNA of its parents but is only one or a few cells compared with a hundred trillion or so in an adult and probably five trillion in a newborn infant.

If a fertilized ovum or an embryo is a "child," is it also an adult? The similarities between a newborn infant and an adult are much less than the differences between a fertilized ovum, an embryo, or an early stage fetus, or an apple seed and an infant.

PROPAGANDA AND SEMANTICS

Semantics is the area of philosophy that deals with the meaning of words or phrases. It deals with "signification"—what is signified or meant by a word. Changing the meaning of a word often helps in a propaganda campaign. Propaganda is a general term meaning to "propagate" or develop an idea or an activity. There are many misused or misunderstood words or phrases used in advertising, political campaigns, wars, and every area in which people are trying to convince others of something.

Sometimes the arguments are logical, clear and truthful meanings, but often they are psychological—geared at the emotions rather that to the intellect. When we appeal to sympathy or fear we are more likely to gain followers or contributions for our cause. When we appeal to pride or patriotism we should also gain followers and converts. Appeals to power sell a lot of beer when the TV sofa athlete can associate with a football hero who drinks the same brew.

The pro-abortion people have successfully used the ideas: of freedom, and that women should have the right to control their own bodies. The anti-abortion leaders have successfully used the ideas that they are "pro-life" and that abortion is "killing a child." We will discuss these in more detail later, but are the pro-abortion people "pro-death?" Of course not! But they have a different definition of when life starts. We will also discuss this at length later. But what about "killing a child?" No dictionary or informed person would define an embryo or fetus as a child. Let us look briefly at the definitions of the stages of human development as defined in the Merriam-Webster dictionary:

Zygote

> a cell formed by the union of two gametes (i.e. a sperm and an ovum)

Embryo

> a vertebrate at any stage of development prior to birth or hatching
> an animal in the early stages of growth and differentiation that are characterized by cleavage, the laying down of fundamental tissues, and the formation of primitive organs and organ systems especially: the developing human individual from the time of implantation to the end of the eighth week after conception
> something as yet undeveloped

Fetus

> an unborn or unhatched vertebrate especially after attaining the basic structural plan of its kind specifically
> a developing human from usually two months after conception to birth

Infant

> a child in the first period of life
> a person not of full age, a minor

Child

> a young person especially between infancy and youth
> a person not yet of age Under the law she is still a child.
> an unborn or recently born person

If a minor can be called an infant, we can equate a teenager with a newborn baby. Are these really the same? The same is true when defining an embryo or fetus as a child. The lack of a precise definition confuses us—as the propagandists fully expect..

Anti-abortion proponents use an inexact meaning of "child," that implies its future state, such as a pregnant mother might say, "My child will have the best of everything." This might even imply that her unborn child will attend Harvard because his ancestors attended the university and his father has given millions to the endowment fund. So "child" in this usage might include the period from embryo to adult.. But we never hear of the "pro-life" people talking about aborting an adult. The point is that there are commonly understood meanings and descriptive words for each stage of development from zygote to senility. For clarity and understanding we should be precise. But to convince the average person, a sleight of tongue may work magic.

The floating zygote should attach to the wall of the uterus within one to two weeks. After a month, it is about the size of a pencil point or an apple seed. At about five weeks it is called an embryo. It then continues to grow and somewhere around eight weeks, as its organs begin to develop, it is called a fetus. At three months, it weighs only about an ounce. It remains a fetus until it is born. Are these sizes such that we can call them unborn children? Are they really only potential children through part or all of the pregnancy?

We should ask, what is it that makes a one-celled zygote equal to a 5 trillion-cell infant? Or what is the difference between a human zygote with 46 chromosomes and a hare or sable antelope with 46 chromosomes? And if chromosomes are the major factor in being human, is it possible that we might be inferior to a pigeon with 80 or a pineapple with 50 chromosomes?

Or, is it only about potential? If so, is it potential for living, for thinking, for communicating, for being positive influences on human society, or even for entering heaven? Certainly, each of us is alive—whether pigeon, pineapple, or person! But a few humans may not have the ability to think or communicate as well as some hares or pigeons. But many humans will contribute either more or less to society than the hare. The human might pollute more or become a criminal, while the hare might make a good meal for a human or contribute a foot or two towards the good luck of some superstitious humans. And if some of the animal rights people are correct, the hares might even find their way to heaven.

In a 1990 Papal audience, Pope John Paul II proclaimed that "the animals possess a soul and men must love and feel solidarity with our smaller brethren." He added that animals are the "fruit of the creative action of the Holy Spirit and merit respect," and that they are "as near to God as men are." But no pope had yet said that animals go to heaven!

However, during a recent public appearance, Pope Francis comforted a boy whose dog had just died, saying, "One day, we will see our animals again in eternity. Paradise is open to all of God's creatures." This can be seen in context—a "white lie" may be the lesser sin when the object of the statement was to comfort a grieving boy. (There is some question about the translation of the statement from Italian to English.) However, in 1990, Pope John Paul II said animals have souls, but didn't say they went to heaven. But then Pope Benedict, gave a 2008 sermon that seemed to say the opposite. Some pastors in other denominations have told people that because animals are God's creations, they too have that spirit of God—a soul. So they too can go to heaven.

So if I go to Hell, I may never see my goldfish again. He has lived a perfect life, swimming in circles. I wonder if in heaven he can swim rectangles or triangles? That's a whale of a question. Can't wait to find out.

What is the difference between being a person and being a potential person? I hear people say that life begins at conception. Is it a human life or a potential human life? What if God decides to start a miscarriage? Is God guilty of murder? If it's not a human life yet, it obviously would not be a murder. Is it a person in the Biblical sense, or are the Jews right that human life starts at birth?

But let us leave the God-based reasons for another chapter. Suffice to say, one can find both sides of most issues in the Bible. One must merely pick and choose the chapter and verse.

WHAT IS A PERSON?

We must define what a person is. Is it a body? A mind? Is it spiritual, being in the image of God? To be a person, is it required to reach a certain intellectual or moral level? Are chimps or dolphins persons? What if they are more intelligent or more moral than some people? If a chimpanzee is more intelligent than some child or adult do we drop the lower achieving *homo sapiens* from our species or do we widen our definition of 'person' to include some of the genus of mammals into personhood?

DEFINITIONS ARE NOT NECESSARILY TRUE

Definitions may depend on the situations in which they are used. For example, we all remember from studying geometry that the shortest distance between two points is a straight line. Of course, Euclid, in developing his definitions and theorems, assumed that space is flat. If we are to look at Einstein's general theory of relativity, we can understand that space, or at least parts of space, are curved. Therefore, the shortest distance between two points would be a curved line. So, the "one size fits all" definition is open to serious questions.

The arguments about abortion often hinge on the definition of life, or of human life. So, in defining various concerns about life we can see quite different aspects of living. Do we mean:

> ➤ Life
> ➤ Meaningful life
> ➤ Human life
> ➤ Meaningful human life

LIFE

Humans are alive. Roses are alive. Monkeys are alive. Ova are alive. Sperm are alive. Most people talking about abortion being murder are only concerned with human life after conception.

Many Hindus believe that all of us are part of the pantheistic god that is the totality of the universe—The Brahman. There are some animals that are particularly sacred, like the cow. Other animals might well be consumed, but not the cow. In the Jain religion, an offshoot of Hinduism, the believers will not eat any animal. So all animals have meaningful life. For most Jews and Christians, animal life is not sacred, so the animals can be consumed.

Are we concerned with all life, all animal life, or all human life? And what makes human life special? Is it that we generally have 46 chromosomes? But, as mentioned, some other animals, like hares, also have 46 chromosomes. Is it our intelligence, which, on the average is greater than other animals? But what about an intelligent chimpanzee or dolphin that is more intelligent than some very low IQ'd people? (Yes, this does happen.) Is it that we are more moral than other animals? But what about the serial killer compared with a dolphin that saves a person's life—it has happened, you know! Is it that humans have God-given souls? But can you prove empirically that God or souls exist?

However, some laws and some religious commandments assume that it is human life. Our question, of course, is when does human life start. Whatever we say, no matter how much we believe it, is only a definition. It is not provable.

"Human life" can be defined as beginning anywhere between conception, when the sperm and ovum meet, to the birth-- or even later. "Quickening," the first movement felt by a mother, has been a traditional definition of life starting, because it could be felt.

BEFORE CONCEPTION (PRE-EXISTENCE)

The idea of preexistence can be traced to the Hindus, to Plato, and into Christianity. The Hindu idea is that everything is God, so we are all part of that infinite "soul." Through reincarnations, our portion of that soul goes through many lives while we attempt to purify our being by eliminating desires (vasanas). When we have eliminated all of our desires we become one with the pantheistic god.

Plato had the idea that we are born with knowledge from our previous lives and we must seek to relearn that knowledge.

The psychologist Carl Gustav Jung, more recently, hypothesized that the deepest part of our mind is a collective unconscious in which we are influenced by the past knowledge of the human race.

The Koran speaks of all souls being created at the time of the creation of Adam.

The Christians, generally, have not accepted this idea that souls existed before conception. However, one of the early "Christian fathers," Origen, quoted both St. Paul and Jeremiah in backing his argument. But his ideas were condemned as heresy at the second Council of Constantinople in 553.

The Christian group that accepts the preexistence of souls is the Church of Jesus Christ of Latter Day Saints. Joseph Smith, its founder, taught that the souls are eternal, just as is God. These souls may learn before birth, but they must acquire a body that could learn more, while experiencing pain and joy so that it can learn the essence of faith. For this reason, Mormons are against abortion because the existing souls need a body to learn the essentials of "faith."

CONCEPTION

In 1869 Pope Pius IX stated that life starts at conception. In 2017, The American College of Pediatricians agreed with the pope.

Huge numbers of fertilized ova never implant. Were they alive? Were they human? Did they die a natural death? Were they aborted by God? If they had souls, where do they go? The Roman Catholic Church has long held that the soul carries the "original sin" from the Garden of Eden, and that the sin of Adam and Eve lives in the soul until baptism, when the sin is washed away. So, unbaptized babies could not go directly to heaven, so rested in Limbo until Judgment Day.

Other religions, like the Christian Orthodox, do not believe in a Limbo.

IMPLANTATION

Under the George W. Bush administration, in 2004, the Unborn Victims of Violence Act, was passed. It implies that life starts when the blastocyst implants in the uterus.

WHEN ARE YOU A PERSON?

Being "alive" and being a "person" may not be the same thing. 1 U.S. Code, para.1 states: "In determining the meaning of any Act of Congress, unless the context indicates otherwise— the words "person" and "whoever" include corporations, companies, associations, firms, partnerships, societies, and joint stock companies, as well as individuals."

So, while we mortals think of a "person" as being a member of the human race of *homo sapiens*, the U.S. government defines it quite differently. You are certainly allowed to define anything the way you want. For semantic clarification, we now understand the government's definition. (So, if you want to define a mosquito as an elephant, or the Twin Towers, or George

Washington—as long as we know the signification of the word "mosquito" in your argument, we don't have a logical problem. But if you were to tell an audience that "on September 11, 2001 terrorists crashed two airliners into a mosquito, or that a mosquito was the first president of the United States—some people might figure that you are a strong candidate for the "funny farm.")

Dictionaries usually cite more than a half dozen definitions for "person." All are likely to be related to a member of the human race. Some dictionaries add a single definition for a single entity, such as a corporation, as is used sometimes in law. Perhaps a phrase such as an "entity involving one or more humans" should be used. As it is, the definition of the U.S. government for "person" does not comport with a "right to life" advocate saying that "abortion is killing a person." If so, is a bankruptcy an abortion of a corporate "person?" And if it is--should it be outlawed? Or is stopping a spinoff of a corporation an abortion? So when Google stopped the operation of Google+, was it an abortion? Of course, then we look at the word "abortion" and it really means "stopping something." Ah, playing with words is not child's play!

Abortion.com writes that: "Every human being is a person. Personhood is properly defined by membership in the human species, not by stage of development within that species."

We find these multiple definitions of terms confusing in personal discussions and in the law courts. In numerous Supreme Court decisions, covering over 100 years, corporations have been judged to be "persons" and "citizens" and therefore allowed free speech, freedom of the press, and freedom of religion. So we must differentiate between a human person and other persons. So, is the "personhood" of corporations and adult humans, also appropriate to zygotes, embryos and blastocysts that are not yet capable of stating opinions or contributing to a society? Many questions, eh?

If a zygote or embryo has a right to life, or to full "personhood," states and municipalities usually have laws that protect children from severe sexual or physical abuse. Does this "person," zygote or embryo, also have the right to a drug- or tobacco-free uterus? Should expectant mothers be jailed for violating that embryo's rights to a healthy environment? Has Kant's requirement to "treat everyone as an end," been violated? Does this "person" have the right to effective parenting?

There are laws that require immunization against certain diseases. Some cases in which adults refuse medical treatment for themselves or their children because of their religious beliefs are often decided against them because the "state has the right and duty to protect its citizens." Should this "right and duty" extend into the womb? The "pro-life" advocates have so far only advocated for life. But the Preamble of the Constitution states that:

"We the people of the United States, in order to form a more perfect union, establish justice, insure domestic tranquility, provide for the common defense, promote the general welfare, and secure the blessings of liberty to ourselves and our posterity, do ordain and establish this Constitution for the United States of America."

Even though the Preamble only indicates the spirit of the law, and is not itself a law, we might ask:

> ➢ Is it "just" to have babies born to parents who don't want them?
> ➢ Is it "just" to have babies born to parents who smoke, knowing the harmful effects of passive smoke?
> ➢ Is it "just" to have children born to alcoholics or to addicts of other drugs?
> ➢ Is it "just" to have children born into poverty when they may be malnourished or deprived of an adequate education?

We can ask the same questions about whether an unwanted child, or a child without a maximum chance at being the best that he or she can be, promotes the general welfare. Some governments have enacted laws that prevent pregnant women from doing harm to their unborns. Smoking, drinking, and other drugs have sometimes been made illegal for pregnant women.

So, when are you a socially adequate person?

MEANINGFUL HUMAN LIFE

"Meaningful human life" may be considered as starting even later than birth. In fact, in countries with capital punishment, a life that once had meaning, now has no meaning. In countries where war is being fought, soldiers may not have meaningful lives because they are sent to die.

In Row v Wade at Point X, "meaningful life" seems to imply that the life would be meaningful to the future child—not meaningful to the society.

"With respect to the State's important and legitimate interest in potential life, the "compelling" point is at viability. This is so because the fetus then presumably has the capability of meaningful life outside the mother's womb. State regulation protective of fetal life after viability thus has both logical and biological justifications. If the State is interested in protecting fetal life after viability, it may go so far as to proscribe abortion during that period, except when it is necessary to preserve the life or health of the mother." (Roe v. Wade 410 U.S. 113, at pg.164)

But then there is infanticide, killing the newborn, it has been practiced for as long as there have been humans—because the parents, or the society, do not see the new lives to be meaningful.

> ➢ It may be used when a mother or father doesn't want the child—a self-centered reason,
> ➢ When the god or gods approve of it, or demand it as a sacrifice—a God-based reason, or
> ➢ When it is used for population control—a society-based reason.

Paleolithic and Neolithic excavations show extensive killing of children. It was, or is, undoubtedly an economic factor in most cases. Although in ancient Sparta it was to make certain that the babies were strong enough to be effective Spartans.

Quite commonly the religion of the people condoned, and even praised the practice, as the little the ones were sacrificed to the gods in various ways—from being tossed over a cliff to being disemboweled in the temple. A recent find in Peru discovered 140 children, as old as 12 killed, and their hearts removed. As we move into the Roman times, population was often controlled by sacrificing the firstborn child to the gods. However, the Romans, in the Second Century, outlawed infanticide, but we have scant records of the law being enforced.

The Jews and early Christians frowned on infanticide, but it still occurred in limited situations. Even into the Middle Ages, it was practiced in some Christian areas.

We do find prophets condemning the practice in Biblical times, although some early church fathers condemned the practice. And it is specifically outlawed in the Koran.

It was more common in older days and has become much less common with modern religions, with the availability of contraception, and abortion. Although we still hear of some young mothers discarding their newborns in trash containers.

In the play, "My Son: The Waiter—a Jewish Tragedy," the main character quotes his mother as saying, "A fetus is not viable until it graduates from medical school."

PERSONHOOD AND RIGHTS

Is the zygote fully possessing of all human rights, including the right to vote? And if it can't read should its parents be allowed to record his vote? Should it be jailed if has absorbed some heroin from its addicted mother? Should this crime be recorded on its criminal record? If it doesn't have any rights, when does it gain them? Does it only have a right to life? And if so why don't all adults have that right: like soldiers drafted into the army who might be killed in a war, doctors who perform abortions and are shot by right-to-lifers, or death row prisoners?

If it has the right to life, does it have the right to the best intrauterine life possible? What if its mother or father smokes? What if its mother is malnourished? What if its mother is a drug addict? Does it have the right to the best childhood possible, with adequate food, education, emotional warmth and love? Should all zygotes be desired by one or both parents?

EFFECTIVE PARENTING.

It takes a masterful, aware, and loving parent to give a child the feeling that he or she is worthwhile and to help that child in overcoming the inferiority complex that was developed in its early years. The key for parents is whether or not they have the ability to love. And of course, what guarantee is there that either wanted, or unwanted, children will be loved. (This will be discussed in the next chapter.) What are the chances that either wanted or unwanted children will be able to develop their abilities and their happiness to the maximum?

AND SO—

As we move through the book, we must be continually aware of the meanings of the key terms in the various arguments. Who is a person? What is life? What is a meaningful life? Who can be a loving parent? Is just being born the major concern of God or society? Which basic assumptions should be primary in the discussion of abortion?

So, should abortion be legal? Let's look at the values involved.

CHAPTER 4 LOOKING AT THE SELF-CENTERED REASONS FOR AND AGAINST ABORTION

There are several questions we must answer if we are to take a self-centered position on abortion—pro or con.

When we are looking at "selfs," we need to look at the pregnant woman, the people who are close to her, like family and friends, and at the "self" of the embryo, both in the uterus and after it is born. We also must look at the immediate time, as well as what might happen in the future. For example, a woman who has had an abortion might wish 30 years later, that she had kept the potential child. And as we will discuss later, there are children and adults who wish they had never been born.

IS MY CONCERN "NOW" OR THE FUTURE?

We can look at self-centered reasons from the point of view of what do I desire today, or what would be good for me in the future. The 25% of pregnancies that end in abortion worldwide are undoubtedly done most often for self-centered reasons. Which are done thinking only of the present inconvenience? Which are done with the future, of either the pregnant woman or the potential child, in mind?

The present versus the future values for my life are constant value choices. For example, there might be a party tonight that I would like to attend, but I have a test tomorrow in a very important college class that may be important for my future. Which do I do? When we are looking at future rewards, we call it "deferred gratification."

> ➢ I will live frugally and get good grades in college, so that I can get the type of job I really want.
> ➢ I will stay on my healthy diet and lose the 40 pounds I gained during the last 15 years.

We see this dilemma over and over again in life.

> - I would like to lose weight, but I want some more cookies.
> - I enjoy driving fast, but the policeman gave me a hundred-dollar ticket yesterday—and I don't have $100.
> - I was sexually excited but did not have a contraceptive, and now I am pregnant.
> - I am very unhappy, should I take an opioid or commit suicide—or see a counsellor?

In terms of abortion, the "now" is usually primary, but the future may be just as important. A woman who has her heart set on finishing school or entering the professional work force may have no plans of ever wanting a child. The "maternal instinct" is not universal! On the other hand, a woman may have plans for motherhood, but not at this stage of her life.

Or what if she is pregnant with twins but only wants one child? This week, the leader of a minor political party in Norway—the Christian Folk Party—said that if a woman can carry one fetus she can certainly carry two. He was quickly corrected by women who had carried twins or triplets. (Gee!, I thought men knew everything.)

On the other side of the coin, there are many who want children, but are biologically incapable of having them. In vitro fertilization is an option, and has resulted in about a hundred thousand American babies and 50,000 British babies. The Catholic Church opposes this method of pregnancy. One wonders why!

WHICH "SELF" IS OF PRIMARY IMPORTANCE—THE MOTHER OR THE EMBRYO?

Most of the current arguments for self-centered reasons for abortion revolve around the mother. Whether she wants the child, has been raped, is a victim of incest, has a right to privacy, or is entitled to her own freedom of choice.

I wonder why the potential child is never considered. As a mental health professional, I am well aware of the many studies, as well as my private observations, that clearly show that many children have not been wanted or effectively loved. These ineffectively loved children are often children who were wanted. We can imagine that unwanted children will have even less of a chance of being loved. And, unloved children are far more prone to make up for that psychological void by joining accepting groups—often anti-social, such as street gangs and terrorist organizations. Prison inmates are nearly universal in relating their negative childhood experiences, from sexual to physical abuse. To make up for their abuse, they adjust to their inferiorities by attacking various elements in their society—by robbing, fighting, bullying, or killing.

Today we find bullying and abusive behavior at every age and in every level of society.

Unloved children don't always attack society. Many unloved children, rather than attacking reality, retreat from it by developing personality problems, illegal drug use, neuroses, psychoses, or by committing suicide.

So let us look a bit at "love" because every child should be loved, but in spite of the nearly universal affirmation of parents that they love their children, it is doubtful that the majority of children have really been loved.

WHAT IS LOVE?

But what is love? We use the term so loosely that it becomes almost meaningless. In fact, most of the time that it is used, it merely means I approve of something-- love my pizza or my partner. This is quite the exact opposite of the meaning of love in the psychological or religious contexts. In these contexts, love is seen more as giving than as being approved of. In the Encyclopedia of Mental Health, Ashley Montagu, perhaps America's major social thinker, was asked to write the chapter on "Love." Naturally he had to first define it. His definition is, by far, the most complete and the most accepted definition of love. It is:

"Love is the communication to another person, of one's deep involvement in that person's welfare, of one's profound interest in him as a person, demonstrated by acts that: support, stimulate, and contribute to the realization of his potential and to the fulfillment of his personality."

DEVELOPING A CHILD'S POTENTIAL

One's potential is strongly associated with overcoming what psychologist Alfred Adler called the inferiority complex. As babies, we have no power. We cannot feed ourselves, talk, or change our own diapers. This develops in us the need for power over our lives.

POWER OVER

You have often heard of the two aspects of power, "power over" or "power to." I am not aware of any studies that indicate how many people have outgrown their need to have "power over." We see it continually in young children. The toddler may cry when he or she cannot get what is desired—and the parents may succumb to the tantrum. In school, bullying is rampant. In the later teen years, or young adulthood, we often find power in joining social or anti-social groups that give us a feeling of control over our childhood inadequacies.

The "Me too" movement is a power reaction to males having used their power over women in the sexual component of our behavior. The Ku Klux Klan, and other far right groups use this "power over" behavior in the racial and religious areas. Bosses may use it in the workplace. Husbands or wives may use it against each other or against their children in the relationship aspects of their lives. It is universal! It is so prevalent that we often think that it is normal behavior. It is common, but is always a symptom of inferiority, and that is not ideal if we want ethical and truly "human" behavior in our society –at every level.

Teenagers can also develop their "power to" by participating in sports, doing well in school, volunteering for worthwhile projects, mastering a musical instrument, etc. Adults may find "power to" in their lives by completing their educations, finding an enjoyable job, creating a successful marriage, building or buying a house, or doing socially valuable enterprises. But often they try to achieve adulthood by behaving immaturely. Getting married, just because it is a relationship reserved for adults is common, and immature. Having a child because it shows that we are adults is another immature action. In 2008 18 classmates at Gloucester High School became pregnant at the same time. A school official said it was a pregnancy pact, but it wasn't. Many didn't know each other. Six had abortions, one child died a "crib death." One other was born 3 months premature and has had severe health problems. Ten are now in the fourth grade with 26-year-old mothers.

People who are successful in business or politics have achieved in this "power to" area, but as we commonly see, many have not outgrown their need for "power over." Harvey Weinstein, although a successful movie mogul, or Donald Trump, as a successful businessman and politician, although unsuccessful as a national president, are prominent examples.

DOES A CHILD DESERVE A LOVING PARENT?

What if the potential child could choose, and realized that it would be unwanted, and possibly severely abused? That of course is a moot point, or maybe a mute point, since the embryo has neither voice nor clairvoyance. But we certainly might assume that it would not have the loving care of a child who was wanted.

Even parents who are greatly concerned about their children, may not have the ability to love in the sense that Montagu outlined. We can assume that unwanted children will have even less opportunity to be loved and fewer chances to conquer their need to fulfill their power needs.

What happens when a person is not loved or made to feel important? Psychologist Erich Fromm made the point clearly that "we learn to love by being loved."

So how much concern do we have for any embryo or fetus, in terms of whether they have a good chance of being loved unselfishly after they are born, as Montagu mentioned.

But since the embryo or fetus does not have a voice, it is the desire of the potential mother that we hear loudly voiced by the "freedom of choice" demonstrators. The woman who does not want a child just now-- or never, is more likely to be uncaring for the child-- and may be resentful through the life of the child. The reasons may vary considerably, from not wanting to be bothered, to not having the necessary financial resources to handle her own desires and the needs of the child, to having more important vocational goals in mind.

Does the potential parent have the present, or future, financial ability to raise a middle-class child? When the Department of Agriculture of the United States tells us that a middle-class child costs $235,000 to raise a child to age 16, this does not include college—should the financial ability of the future parent or parents be a concern for the unborn? Similar statistics in the UK are that it costs 231,000 British Pounds ($295,000) to raise a child to the age of 21.

(You might want to study the topic of "love" in "Love—the You, the Me, the Us" by the author.)

What if genetic testing or ultrasound examinations showed the embryo or fetus to be disabled or carrying a very negative genetic trait. Will this be a happy child?

LET'S LOOK AT THE POSITIONS PEOPLE TAKE DEPENDING ON THEIR DIFFERENT BASIC ASSUMPTIONS.

A major psychological reason, for not having an abortion, is often used by those against the procedure. They assert that the pregnant woman will regret her action. But two recent studies indicate that this is seldom a factor. One study shows that 95% of women who have had an abortion do not regret it. The other study showed it to be 99% who had no regrets.

HOW TRUE IS THE EVIDENCE WE HEAR?

Both sides of the abortion position have been known to present evidence of studies done to validate their positions. They may cite studies done by advocates of their positions who have manipulated the evidence. They may cite only partial evidence or findings from legitimate studies. They may cite studies of populations that are too small to prove anything. They may cite studies of populations far different from yours. They may cite studies from non-experts or charlatans. They may cites from questionable journals. Here are some commonly cited studies.

A Chinese study published in an Indian journal reported an increased risk of breast cancer in women who had had abortions in China. This was quickly circulated by those opposed to abortion.

But then, The American Cancer Society, the National Cancer Institute, the American College of Obstetricians and Gynecologists, and the National Health Service of the United Kingdom all refuted the claim that abortion can lead to a higher probability of developing breast cancer. A fertility investigation of 10,767 women by the joint Royal College of General Practitioners and the Royal College of Obstetricians and Gynecologists found that women who had at least two abortions experienced the same future fertility as those who had at least two natural pregnancies.

Can abortions cause psychological damage. Anti-abortion advocates have cited a peer-reviewed study published in the Scandinavian Journal of Public Health and stated that young adult women who undergo abortion may be at increased risk for subsequent depression. What they don't tell you is that teenage girls who had abortions showed no depression. Another important factor is that the subjects were all from Norway, so the effect might be greater or less when compared to New York, Nebraskan, or Nevada women. A major detriment of this study, and all similar studies, is that the evaluative tools used to measure depression after childbirth or abortion were not used before the pregnancy. This, of course, would be next to impossible to do, unless all women in the country were administered this depression measuring tool every year—or every month. Then, we should also know the marital status, the emotional attachment to the potential father, etc.

A peer-reviewed study published in BMC Medicine found that women who underwent an abortion had significantly higher anxiety scores on the hospital anxiety and depression scale up to five years after the pregnancy termination. It might be noted that BMC Medicine is a journal that requires payment in order to publish the article. This is generally $3000 per article. Because of this, the quality of the articles is much more likely to be inferior to those in more reputable journals. Reputable journals do not require authors to pay for publication.

The BMC Medicine study involved 40 women who had suffered miscarriages and 80 who had undergone abortions. The study was done among patients in one hospital in Norway. It found that women who had suffered miscarriages had greater distress in the immediate time following the occurrence. However, in the long term, those who underwent abortions had greater feelings of guilt than the miscarriage group. As you might imagine, what happens in a small hospital in Norway may not be representative of women in high society in France, in poor villages in India, or for the average American woman.

A peer-reviewed study published by the Southern Medical Journal of more than 173,000 American women found that women who aborted were 154% more likely to commit suicide than women who carried to term. The study looks impressive to begin with because the number of women in the study was 173,000. What the paragraph does not mention is that they were all poor women in California who were using the government paid Medicaid insurance. Would study apply to middle class women in Chicago or London? The study was reported by a strong Catholic antiabortion person, Doctor D.C. Reardon. Reardon has an electrical engineering degree from the University of Illinois and a non-accredited doctorate from a "degree mill" in Hawaii-- that requires no coursework, only money.

A study published in the highly respected British Medical Journal reported that the mean annual suicide rate amongst women who had an abortion was 34.7 per 100,000, compared with a mean rate of 11.3 per 100,000 in the general population of women. That's kind of scary! But wait!

It is a comprehensive study of Finnish women. For Finland, it may be highly representative. But, as you may know, people living in the far north, particularly Sweden, Norway, and Finland, have more than the normal amount of depression because of seasonal affective disorder, because of the lack of sunshine during the winter. This tends to make depression more common in Nordic countries. In Norway, many from the north are sent to the sun the Canary Islands for a week or two, at national expense as a prevention for seasonal affective disorder. So, this very important study may have limited validity outside of Finland, or the Nordic countries.

A caution on believing what you read in peer reviewed journals:

- Both sides of the abortion issue, as in most other ethical questions, generally cite studies that validate their positions. When reading opinions that are backed up by citations in journals, don't believe all you read. Check the original article on the Internet.

- What is the quality of the journal. BMJ, the British Medical Journal is a very high quality journal in which the best articles are chosen and there is no charge to the authors. BMC Medical is a much lower quality journal that charges authors over $3000 to print their article.

- Discern the quality of the authors by finding their academic connections.

- Do the authors have possible biases? An author at a Catholic or evangelical university might well have prejudices against abortion that might prejudice the design of the study or influence how they treat the results. The same might be done by pro-abortion institutions.

- Who are the subjects of the study—social class, religious preferences, geographical location, level of education, age, marital status, etc.

- What is the size of the sample of the subjects in the study? If you are studying Siamese twins or the number of injuries by stepping on land mines while walking around San Francisco, the number will be very small. But if you are determining the death rate for heart attacks, people who have had abortions, or have died during childbirth the numbers should be upward of 40,000. One widely quoted anti-abortion study on depression among those who had had abortions had 40 subjects. The findings in that study were the exact opposite of the country's national studies. In studies using "meta-analyses (studying a large number of studies to ascertain whether there were similar outcomes) various studies found both more, and less, depression after an abortion compared with women who had not been pregnant, women who had had miscarriages, and women who had given birth. The characteristic most commonly found to predict depression after an abortion was previous mental problems and illegal drug use.

➤ Do the subjects come from a background that might influence how they might feel about abortion. Studying the effects of depression after abortions would likely be very different in an evangelical community in Kansas than among atheists in a secular city like New York or Los Angeles.

➤ How were the depressive reactions measured? Post-partum depression is common among women who have given birth. Was it greater or less among women who had opted for abortion?

ABORTION IS HAS VALUE FROM THE SELF-CENTERED VIEWPOINT OF THE WOMAN

The battle cry of the self-centered proponents is that women have the right to choose. The pregnant woman may decide based on her present circumstances. She may be in school or in a job that she enjoys. She may feel that a pregnancy and motherhood will negatively affect her social life.

She may already have one, or more, children and believe that one more child will require too much additional work or money.

Poor unmarried women, and even married women, generally prefer an abortion to having to devote twenty years or more of caring for a 'love child'. The financial, economic and emotional needs of the child generally fall on the mother—and when abortion is available, it is usually her choice. Even in Catholic Latin-American countries, the poor generally opt for pregnancy termination through pills, coat hangers, or surgical inducement. Illegal clinics may charge the poor women high fees for abortions. But it is worth the cost for most, if they can find the money. Pills of many sorts can upset the body's metabolism enough to cause a miscarriage, so they tend to be the method used when the self-interested pregnant woman confronts a religious anti-abortion rule.

In the U.S., most of the abortions are performed on women over 25, and 60% of them already have children. It seems strange that mothers with children aren't more adept at using contraception.

However, most of these said that they wanted to give their children the best possible life and another child would take from her existing children. The majority are white, and as you might expect, more than 4 out of 5 are unmarried. Should more teenagers have abortions to save their children from being raised by immature mothers?

About 700 mothers die each year in the U.S. due to pregnancy or delivery complications, and African-American women are four times more likely to be victims than white women.

SAFETY—DANGER TO HER HEALTH

There is also a safety reason for having an abortion, in that an abortion is far safer than giving birth. This would probably be far down most women's lists, but for some, with anatomical or physiological problems that would make childbirth a major medical risk, it might be a consideration.

Here are the facts. A woman's risk of dying from having an abortion is 0.6 in 100,000, while the risk of dying from giving birth is around 14 times higher (8.8 in 100,000). The mortality rate of undergoing a colonoscopy is more than 40 times greater than that of an abortion.

Modern abortion procedures are safe and do not cause lasting health issues such as cancer and infertility. A peer-reviewed study published in Obstetrics & Gynecology reported that less than one quarter of one percent of abortions lead to major health complications. The study also found that pregnancy-related complications were more common with childbirth than with abortion. The American Medical Association and the American College of Obstetricians and Gynecologists stated that abortion is one of the safest medical procedures performed in the United States.

HEALTH PROBLEMS

A factor well known to psychologists, is that a major way that insecure females look for validation and approval is through sex, often promiscuous sex. So, mental problems, commonly precede the impregnation—and the abortion.

Another study, often cited, deals with the effects on men of their partner's abortion. The study involved only 72 couples.

Still, the choice over when and whether to have children is central to a woman's independence, mental health, and her ability to determine her future. Reproductive choice empowers women by giving them control over their own bodies. Former Supreme Court Justice Sandra Day O'Connor wrote in the 1992 decision in Planned Parenthood v. Casey, "The ability of women to participate equally in the economic and social life of the nation has been facilitated by their ability to control their reproductive lives." Supreme Court Justice Ruth Bader Ginsburg wrote in her dissenting opinion in Gonzales v. Carhart (2007) that "undue restrictions on abortion infringe upon a woman's autonomy to determine her life's course, and thus to enjoy equal citizenship stature." The case dealt with one method of partial birth abortions passed under the Bush administration. It was a 5 to 4 decision.)

ABORTION DOES NOT HAVE VALUE) FROM A SELF-CENTERED POINT OF VIEW

"Now on the other side of the issue. She might say, I might later regret not having the child. Perhaps as I grow older I might wish that I had someone related to me to talk to and to love. In that case, my abortion would not have had value from my self-centered point of view. So, the abortion might have had value for me when I was younger, but not have value for me today.

On the other hand, you don't have to have a blood relative to have a companion. In fact, I would guess that having a longtime friend might be more of a companion than a person many years younger who might well have a life of her own to create.

Millions of American women have aborted a child, and in some, the pain, loss, and emotional need to justify what was done, both on the part of the mother and on the part of her loved ones, is strong and deep. This means that, in any debate, you may face an invisible thumb on the scale.

As you might expect, bleeding or infection can result, just as in any operation. Excessive bleeding occurs about once every thousand abortions. But, compared with the risks and expenses of raising an unwanted child, these complications are generally minor.

WHAT ABOUT POSSIBLE MENTAL PROBLEMS AS A RESULT OF AN ABORTION?

On the other side of the issue, we can criticize some of the pro-abortion studies. The American Psychiatric Society, in 2018, reported several studies which did not bear out the findings and conclusions of the studies listed above. Studies on both sides of the issue have been criticized for sometimes shoddy scholarly work. The mental health of the woman prior to pregnancy, and the shock of learning that she was pregnant, can increase the anxiety and depression which may be felt during or after an abortion-- or after childbirth. There may be many other issues that make a pregnancy desired or undesirable because of one's educational or vocational goals, one's relationship status, one's prior or present mental health status, etc.

With so many variables it is well-nigh impossible to match women in a population according to their poverty level, how they feel about that poverty, the emotional attachment they may have had to the man who impregnated her, and a great many other factors in her life such as her education goals or her aspirations in the workplace.

Those arguing against abortion because it may cause mental problems in the mother are countered with a major study by the American Psychological Association in 2009 on mental health problems in those who had had abortions and those who had delivered full-term. They found no difference. Multiple abortions, on the other hand, may indicate the propensity to more mental health problems, although the reasons for them are likely to be associated more with their propensity to get pregnant rather than to the abortion. People with low self-esteem and other mental problems may use sex as a way to show that they are desirable and worthwhile. Then if pregnancy occurs, one more mental health issue appears.

Some women will show sadness before or after the procedure. These were found to be generally: the stigma attached to having an abortion; a prior history of mental health problems; personality problems such as low self-esteem; and other factors related to the pregnancy—such as desiring the pregnancy but being influenced by others to terminate the pregnancy.

If the aborted fetus would have become a very positive influence on the world in areas such as science, literature or in the government and would have been a great joy to the mother, this hypothetical child would give a hypothetical reason for the abortion not having value for either the mother or the society. So, if we had two top level NASA scientists who were both psychologically normal. and both capable of loving, in the sense that Montagu envisioned and they were the potential parents of this hypothetical future child perhaps should not be aborted.

CHILD'S POINT OF VIEW—ABORTION HAS VALUE

A baby should not come into the world unwanted. Having a child is an important decision that requires consideration, preparation, financial means, and planning. The Colorado Department of Public Health and Environment stated that unintended pregnancies are associated with birth defects, low birth weight, maternal depression, increased risk of child abuse, lower educational attainment, delayed entry into prenatal care, a high risk of physical violence during pregnancy, and reduced rates of breastfeeding.

WRONGFUL BIRTH

In some jurisdictions, the child, or the child and the parents, can sue the doctors or hospital for not discovering a birth defect. California, The Netherlands, India, and previously Israel, allow for "wrongful life" actions when children are born with disabilities, or otherwise lived unhappy lives.

In 2019, a businessman in Mumbai, India sued his lawyer parents saying that he should not have to suffer through life because of society's problems just because his parents wanted a few moments of pleasure.

"Wrongful life" or "wrongful birth" are the legal terms most commonly used where a child or the child's legal guardian sues the parents, the doctors, or the medical personnel involved in a birth that the offspring believes to be not in his or her interest. It may be because of faulty genetic testing, examinations during pregnancy, or being brought into a world which was not comfortable.

Such legal actions have been used in Israel by a number of disabled people who felt that their lives were miserable because of the birth. Some sued their parents. Some sued the medical profession. Parents also have been involved as plaintiffs against doctors or hospitals because they were not notified of potential genetic problems.

The Supreme Court of Israel has now made it illegal to sue for wrongful birth. The Supreme Court of California, however, has allowed it. In the 1982 case of Curlander v Bio-Science Laboratories, was a case in which the child was born with Tay-Sachs disease when the parents relied on the genetic testing of the laboratory and were not given the correct information, so did not proceed with amniocentesis. The Court's opinion included this paragraph:

"The reality of the 'wrongful-life' concept is that such a plaintiff both exists and suffers, due to the negligence of others. It is neither necessary, nor just, to retreat into meditation on the mysteries of life. We need not be concerned with the fact that had defendants not been negligent, the plaintiff might not have come into existence at all. The reality of genetic impairment is no longer a mystery. In addition, a reverent appreciation of life compels recognition that plaintiff, however impaired she may be, has come into existence as a living person with certain rights." (106 Cal Ap 3d 83)

The Curlander decision gives interested readers an extensive history of the cases in the U.S. that involve "wrongful life."

A similar case had a similar conclusion in New York, but it was overruled by the Supreme Court of New York. Many other states and countries have taken the same route, in disallowing wrongful birth actions. In Germany, the Federal Constitutional Court ruled that "the life of the disabled person is as valuable as a non-disabled person. because, human dignity is a basic concept in the German Constitution." But, the theoretical rationalization probably does not adequately comfort an unhappy, or miserable, living person.

In 2005, the Dutch Supreme Court upheld a lower court decision for a verdict for wrongful life.

Some courts have held that "nonexistent persons" do not have rights. This would of course indicate that life does not start until sometime after conception. In Israel, 600 cases for wrongful birth had been heard before the concept was made illegal.

In the Indian case the plaintiff's mother said that she "would destroy him in court."

In the UK. a report by a cross-party committee found that almost one-in-five children under the age of 15 are growing up in a home that has "limited access to food ... due to lack of money or other resources." The 56-page report added. Yet, Britain is the world's fifth-richest country.

If you would like to read more on this subject, I suggest the book, "Better Not to Have Been: the Harm of Coming into Existence," by David Benatar.

Then, we might look at the Preamble to our Constitution, which sounds good but cannot be used in court. We will quote it again. "We the people of the United States, in order to form a more perfect union, establish justice, insure domestic tranquility, provide for the common defense, promote the general welfare, and secure the blessings of liberty to ourselves and our posterity, do ordain and establish this Constitution for the United States of America."

We therefore might ask:

> Is it "just" to have babies born to parents who don't want them?
> Is it "just" to have babies born to parents who smoke, knowing the harmful

effects of passive smoke?

> Is it "just" to have children born to alcoholics or to addicts of other drugs?

> Is it "just" to have children born into poverty when they may be malnourished or deprived of an adequate education?

We can ask the same questions about whether an unwanted child, or a child without a maximum chance at being the best that he or she can be, promotes the general welfare.

ABORTION DOES NOT HAVE VALUE FROM THE POTENTIAL CHILD'S VIEWPOINT

I'm kind of glad that I wasn't aborted. But then, I'm sure my mother never considered it. I have enjoyed my life immensely—except a couple of times.

But we don't have a crystal uterus to tell us the future of every embryo. I've known some who committed suicide and others who have been happy and productive citizens. I've seen people from apparently loving families produce depressed offspring, and people from unhappy lives in the barrios and ghettos become well-adjusted happy and successful people. But the odds strongly suggest that like produces like. So we can't know for certain the outcome of every unwanted pregnancy.

THE QUESTION OF PAIN

Pain may be felt during the abortion. Several medical specialists have hypothesized that the embryo or fetus feels pain. Some believe that there might be pain as early at 8 weeks, others conclude that it would be at 20 weeks—and it might be severe pain.

Some might ask, if it is more in amplitude and in length of time than the mother will feel in giving birth?

Some states have added laws to require doctors to tell women that the fetus will feel pain during the procedure. Again, we have legislators, who are not neuro-scientists, stating as fact, a belief that is not true. Medical researchers are not certain if and when pain may occur, but legislators are. Let me play the 'devil's advocate' here for a minute.

Is it pain, or only human pain, with which we are concerned?

> Do animals feel pain? Obviously. Have you ever seen an injured dog? How about a fish that is still on the hook?

> Do plants feel pain? No. They have no nervous system. They do sense pressure. And like animals, are made of atoms and molecules powered by electricity.

> Some people choose pastimes where they may endure pain. Strength training and marathon runs are examples.

- Sometimes the government requires pain, or possible pain-- as when draftees undergo painful training, then are sent to war and may be injured or killed.
- Sometimes we choose to inflict or suffer pain in a recreational activity such as in football, boxing, or wrestling.
- Some people even spank their children occasionally.

So is all pain bad? Is only non-volunteered pain bad? Is only human pain bad?

It is said that soldiers feel pain when shot, but that doesn't stop religious people from going to war. Just how much pain might a fetus feel, if it does feel pain. And for how long does that pain last. And compared to the pain it might well feel if brought up in a situation where it was not loved and cared for—which is the greater and more long-standing pain? And, of course, the mother will feel pain, often excruciating, when giving birth—and that pain will last far longer than any pain a fetus might feel for a second or two.

We might even ask if all pain is bad. If my wife pinches me on the cheek to show she loves me. Is that bad? What about a ball carrier in American football being tackled? What about doing sit ups until your abdominal muscles are burning? What about your stomach growling when you are hungry? Is there good pain, natural pain, and bad pain? How do we define it? Where do we draw the line?

Are any legislators passing laws that require the president or the military officers to tell recruits or draftees that they might feel pain during their training or on the battlefield? Is it required of restaurant owners to warn their patrons that they might get food poisoning and be sick? This is to say nothing of your visit to the dentist!!

Perhaps that doesn't go far enough. If pain is a crucial consideration do we need laws to require the butcher to tell customers that chickens and cows experience pain when they are killed. And, sport coaches should tell their athletes that they may feel excruciating pain when running or swimming in a race, when tackling or being tackled in football, or when being elbowed in basketball. And parents who spank their children should advise the child that it hurts them more than it hurts the kid. And what about being warned about the psychological pain caused by tax collectors, judges, or people who refuse to date you!"

It is just another example of not being consistent in our thinking. This is particularly true for legislators who believe that they need to scratch the itch of the voter rather than to develop laws that are intelligent and consistent.

CHAPTER 5   RELIGION AND ABORTION

It is the rule, rather than the exception, that people believe what their priests, ministers, rabbis, imams, or other spiritual advisors say today. But is this the path that their religion has always followed. Gather a group of learned people from any sect and you have a good chance that their opinions on abortion or other moral questions will vary considerably. And if you were able to meet a large group of past prelates in your time machine, the variation would be even greater. The social and economic needs pressing on individuals and societies can influence the way religions are interpreted--and followed. Just look at the way that Catholic Popes have shifted from time to time, relative to when the body's physical cells were ensouled—received their souls.

ABORTION HAS VALUE FROM A GOD-BASED VIEWPOINT

Western religions have never been for abortion as a moral ideal, but often they have not been against it, either. So, let us look at abortion as not necessarily being evil. The major questions for monotheism relative to abortion are:

> ➢   Do we have a soul? And if so, when does the soul enter the body?

> ➢   If the pregnancy is terminated naturally, by a miscarriage, or through an induced abortion--where does the soul go if the embryo or fetus had a soul?

Then we should understand the historical path of our position. We often think that history backs up our quest for justice. But often history is quite different from what we imagine. A confident preacher may shout his demands for action, which he thinks are eternal truths, while ignorant of the oceans of opinions from the past. Will his fiery oratory evaporate the oceans of history—and will we believe that a new truth has emerged from the voice of Vesuvius?

The history of religious ideas has not been as solid and concrete as the cathedrals and mosques that were built to house them.

ENSOULMENT IS A KEY TO PERSONHOOD AND THE MORALITY OF ABORTION

If God puts a soul into every fertilized ovum at the time of conception, or at some later date during the pregnancy, a case can be made that aborting that Image of God, could be murder. Let us look at a few possibilities for such ensoulment.

A major church father, Thomas Aquinas, believed, with his hero Aristotle, that boy babies got their souls forty days after conception and girl babies got theirs ninety days after conception. And if that is true then aborting a male before 40 days or a female before 90 days would not be killing a person. So, it wouldn't be an abortion.

Maybe we should clarify this. It's true that Aquinas did not believe that the soul was transmitted in the semen but was created by God. He seemed to buy into Aristotle's idea that there are three souls, the nutritive, the sensitive and the intellectual. Aquinas believed that a nutritive, or vegetative, soul is there from the beginning, but the intellectual soul is created by God at the end of human generation, those are the forty and ninety day periods mentioned. After that the two previous souls became one with the intellectual soul so that only a single soul exists. But although he was a highly influential church father his views were never accepted as church dogma for eternity like the truths of the resurrection of Jesus or the belief in the Holy Trinity. But the fact is that from the earliest days, most Christian writers have been against abortion. It was murder to kill a woman with child.

It seems that whenever people get together, differences of opinion are the order of the day. Whether they are aligned at the roulette table choosing red or black, at the coffee machine choosing sugar or cream, betting on the home team or the visitors, or in the church or synagogue debating when a future *homo sapiens* gets a soul. It seems that the farther the issue is from empirical verification the louder and more certain become the voices of the guessers.

In the area of ensoulment, it is not so much Jews versus Christians but rather conservatives versus liberals. Without scientific certainty or clear passages from scripture we can find believers of all hues arguing about when the souls were created—Some believe that:

➤ The soul arrived with the sperm, or

➤ God created it at the instant that the sperm wiggled into the ovum, or

➤ It was created a number of days after conception, or

➤ It appeared upon birth, or

➤ It entered the body sometime after birth, as seemed to have happened to Adam and Eve.

Then there is the question as to whether we even have souls.

Jacques Maritain, the eminent Catholic philosopher, said many years ago that "To admit that the human fetus receives the intellectual soul from the moment of its conception, when matter is in no way ready for it, sounds to me like a philosophical absurdity. It is as absurd to call a fertilized ovum a baby." Of course, Jacques was not the Pope!

If we insist on discussing scriptural citings, we again see the futility of appealing to the authority of religion and all the problems that this involves. It is clear that outside philosophical speculation has played a profound role in interpreting what the phrase 'the Image of God' means. We might as well rely on our own analysis for defining what is a person.

What if the soul is infused by God early in the pregnancy, since about a quarter of all human fertilizations end in natural abortions (miscarriages), isn't God the major cause of abortions?

Non-Christian Ideas of Ensoulment

The Koran, as the Bible, is not clear on the morality of abortion if the father or mother wants it. The Koran is clear that if you want to keep the embryo or fetus, you should. But if there is a danger to the mother, abortion is acceptable because the adult woman is more important than the embryo. Killing children, however, is certainly wrong according to Surahs 6:151 and 17:31.

Islam has traditionally regarded 'personhood' as something acquired prior to birth, although Muslims have not always agreed as to when that occurs. Several medieval Muslim authorities mentioned "ensoulment" occurring after 120 days of gestation, or about four months into a pregnancy. This probably relates to the 'quickening' of life that some mothers may experience about that time. Some believed that abortion was murder after this time. Some thought that any abortion was murder.

As with other religions, the Hindus have proponents on both sides of the issue. Since some believe that the newly conceived zygote has already received its soul from someone who has recently died, based on their belief in reincarnation, an abortion at any time would be murder. But others believed that the new soul didn't arrive for three to five months after conception.

Propagating the Faithful

Most of the thinking against abortion would come from religions and their reflection of what is traditional or good for the society—or for increasing of the numbers of members of the church. This is especially true when there are competing religious sects. Look at the anti-abortion approach of the Mormons among the other Christian faiths in America. Look at the Catholics in their battle for souls with the Muslims in Africa, or with the Evangelical Protestants in Latin America.

There seem to be a couple of major reasons. One is that religions tend to protect the status quo of society and of their traditions. The major question from a monotheistic religious position is whether or not there is a soul in the embryo or the fetus when it is aborted. Still, highly respected religious leaders, including two Nobel laureates, have opened the door to admit abortion in some circumstances. But they both are obviously using self-centered and society-based reasons for their decisions. Anglican Bishop Desmond Tutu supported the South African constitutional provision legalizing abortion. And the Dalai Lama, while generally opposed to abortion, said that, 'I think abortion should be approved or disapproved according to the circumstances.

There are now about 400,000 Christian missionaries, including 120,000 Mormons, wandering the world preaching their generally fundamentalist views. This missionary work may increase the anti-abortion sentiment among their converts.

ABORTION BEFORE VIABILITY MAY BE MORAL

If the first breath is the when the soul is imparted, then abortion before birth would be acceptable. In the Bible we read: "And the Lord God formed man of the dust of the ground, and breathed into his nostrils the breath of life; and man became a living soul." (Gen 2:7)

Various points during fetal development have been suggested as significant stages at which simple biology gives way to full personhood. The U.S. Supreme Court decision of Roe v Wade in 1973 chose viability. Today's conservative Christians and Jews insist that it is the moment of conception. Historical Christianity chose animation in the womb, while historical Judaism opted for ensoulment at birth. And the more liberal people in these religions may even wonder if the soul is important. Let us look at each of these concepts for their philosophical merit.

Some of the early Catholic theologians believed that abortion, at least before the fetus quickened, was not murder. In the Eighth Century in England and Ireland an abortion carried a much lighter sentence than did murder or other sins. Oral sex carried a seven-year penance while abortion was only four months. And in the late 16th Century Pope Gregory XIV wrote that the penalty for abortion before ensoulment shouldn't be any more than civil law called for. And civil law was not harsh at that time.

THE MOTHER'S LIFE AS SUPERIOR TO THE EMBRYO OR FETUS

Some thought abortion was OK to save the mother. From the 14th to the 18th century a number of theologians and saints had the same idea. John of Naples, Tomas Sanchez, and Alphonsus Liguri are examples. The Vatican, in the past, has allowed abortion if there was cancer in the uterus or if there was an ectopic pregnancy with the embryo attached to a fallopian tube rather than the uterine wall. Some thought it OK if the fetus had not quickened. Some, such as Augustine, Popes Pius the 9th and the 11th and John Paul II were among these.

In Exodus 21:22-25, the crime of causing a woman to miscarry is treated as a property crime, whereas killing the woman is considered murder and is punished with the death penalty.

HUMANS IN THE IMAGE OF GOD

But let's come back to the 'Image of God' idea. When Genesis tells us that God made man in His image. Does that mean that God has two arms and two legs? Or if God is only spirit, is it the spirit in humans that makes them in the image of God? Or does the newly discovered Assyrian inscription at Tell-Fekheriyeh indicate that it was man's dominion over the animals, as God has dominion over the earth, that makes man in the image, or in the shadow of God. Does the Bible verse give humans a political right rather than a spiritual kinship? Western religious theorists however have opted to give themselves the highest spiritual essence.

In spite of adults being made in the image of God, Jewish tradition has not given that status to a fetus. Their tradition even required abortion to save the life of the mother. This idea of the Jews was similar to that of the Romans and Stoics, that the fetus was a part of the mother, not an independent self. Under Judaism, abortion was certainly not desirable but it was not murder. But they were more restrictive than other religions that were around 2000 years ago.

THE SCRIPTURES AND ABORTION

Since the Scriptures are silent in defining when one becomes a person, it has been left to the theologians to debate with fury when that invisible soul entered the unseen embryo or fetus. Meanwhile the people did what made economic sense to them. The traditional patriarchal power of the Romans survived in Medieval England and allowed a father to kill any child who had not yet tasted food. Infanticide was rife, when children were economic anchors. The infinitesimal worth of the infant allowed him to be left in the forest, ignored, or sold into slavery by his Christian Catholic parents.

Abortion is not specifically against the Ten Commandments. But by inference it might be murder. It is not specifically against the precepts of the Sermon on the Mount. And we might ask why did God allow the technology to perform abortions if He doesn't want them?

OVERPOPULATION AS A THREAT TO LIFE AND TO THE OPPORTUNITY TO ACHIEVE HOLINESS

Indeed, in mainline Christianity, fairly widespread support exists for population stabilization and for family planning and even abortion, as necessary, to save the planet. For many Christians, it is not a women's-rights issue, but an overpopulation issue. And nebulous ideas such as questions of whether a soul is made in the image of God are left to theologians who can add such questions to the other enduring questions of theology, like how many angels can dance on the head of a pin.

AND WHAT ABOUT RELIGIOUS WOMEN?

Religious women may have abortions for self-centered reasons that are counter to their religious views, or they believe that abortion is moral, as we have just discussed.

Women who obtain abortions represent every religious affiliation. 13% of abortion patients describe themselves as "born-again" or Evangelical Christians. And while 21% of Americans are Catholic, 27% of abortion patients are Catholic.

Relative to several official points of view on this subject, many religious organizations and people of faith support women's reproductive rights--The United Methodist Church, The Presbyterian Church, and The Unitarian Universalist Association of Congregations are all officially pro-choice.

Although the Catholic and Lutheran churches are against abortion, many of their members believe abortion should be legal in all or most cases.

For Catholics 51% believe it should be legal in all or most cases. 45% disagreed. For Lutherans, it was 48% to 45%.

And what if the child is to be born into an environment where he or she may sin? With so many people being born into poverty or into unhappy homes, what if they curse God because of their plight. Doesn't taking the Lord's name in vain send you to the devil for all eternity? I don't want to sound like I'm beating a dead zygote here, but is it really so important to have so many souls born?"

ABORTION DOES NOT HAVE VALUE FROM A GOD-BASED POINT OF VIEW

The belief that abortion is always or usually immoral, generally is based on the time the soul enters the body. There is nowhere near universal agreement on when it happens. But before we discuss when it might happen, we should probably define what it is. And here we have more disagreement. Often in the Bible, "soul" seems to mean "mind," as was the common Greek perception. And remember, the early Christian scriptures were generally written in Greek. But now "soul" is commonly understood to mean that spiritual part of a person that is in the Image of God.

Aristotle said it was the 'whatness' of something, the essential nature of it. He said we had three different souls or three levels of soul. The most primitive level of soul is the nutritive which involves nutrition and reproduction. Both plants and animals may have this kind of soul. The next level of soul, is sensory and locomotion. Most animals have this. And, the highest level is intellectual. St. Thomas Aquinas, of all people, said that "the soul is not the substance of God. 'To say that the soul is of the Divine substance involves a manifest improbability. . . and therefore, it is evidently false that the soul is of the substance of God" But whatever it is, for the religions of the Mid-East it is the soul that creates the great canyon between humans and other animals.

Tertullian, often considered the father of Latin Christianity, had the idea that the soul accompanied the biological material of the parents into the womb. Augustine didn't like that idea because it didn't fit with his ideas of Original Sin, so Tertullian's idea was judged to be heresy. If Tertullian's views had been accepted, abortion would have definitely been immoral.

For Hindus, the Kaushitaki Upanishad, from about 500 BCE, states that abortion is equivalent to killing one's parents. And that, you might guess, is a major NO! NO!

Theologians are interesting to read, but Catholic teaching should not be based on the musings of theologians unless the ideas of these theologians have been confirmed by the Church. Pius IX's declaration in 1869, making abortion a capital crime, was merely the formal act verifying the opinions of many concerning the sin of abortion throughout the Church's history. It was added to Canon Law in 1917. Now Pope Benedict XVI has affirmed that stand. In 2006, he reaffirmed Catholic teaching that life begins at the moment of conception, saying embryos are 'sacred and inviolable' even before they become implanted in a mother's uterus. He also said that embryos have rights from conception on.

It seems that the Catholic position on ensoulment comes from a combination of Biblical and papal interpretations. Since the soul was present in the first cell, when the sperm met the ovum, is the soul in every body cell? If so when a surgeon removes an organ, is he murdering? Is it the same as abortion? Could your appendix be in Hell before you die?

When the soul enters the ovum, the embryo, the fetus, or the infant, is critical for many people's idea of the morality of abortion. The Catholic Church holds that in vitro fertilization is immoral, but the Pope did not make a distinction between conception inside or outside of the fallopian tubes or the uterus. When people use such artificial insemination is the soul infused in the fertilized ovum in the test tube or in a Petri dish? We looked at that possibility earlier.

Another question, since about half of fertilized ova never attach to the uterine walls do they also have souls? What about spontaneous miscarriages? Is it fair that the soul of a miscarried embryo gets to go to heaven without ever having to prove itself worthy by living on the earth and doing good works, while the rest of us are trying to "love our neighbors as ourselves?"

And since twins can be a single cell for up to twenty days after conception, does the original fertilized ovum start with two souls at conception, or is a new one added when the embryo splits? If a person were cloned when would the soul be added, or would it be split? Or would the new body not have a soul because every DNA sample gets only one soul?

So now are we to believe that Catholics get their souls at the instant of conception. Protestants may get theirs any time from conception to birth. Muslim embryos get theirs sometime between 6 days and four months. Jewish children get theirs when they are born. So abortions could be moral or immoral depending on a lot of beliefs. But can we find an empirical fact here? Anywhere? I doubt that God will adjust His soul making to the varying opinions of His believers!

The Pope says the fertilized ovum already has a soul. If this is true we would assume that any spontaneous abortion or miscarriage should be welcomed because the zygote's or embryo's soul goes to heaven. But if it is a Catholic zygote's soul it has had several possible destinations because while it hadn't had a chance to sin. Yet, it carried the Original Sin of Adam, because he ate the forbidden fruit of the Tree of Knowledge. From the time of St. Augustine, about 400 AD, the soul went to hell. After Aquinas, 800 years later, it went to Limbo. Limbo was on the border of either heaven or hell, depending on which theologian you read. Now with Pope Benedict XVI's possible disbelief in Limbo we're not sure where it goes. Poor Catholic zygote!

Is it possible that we don't get souls until we are adults? Adam and Eve were created as adults in the image of God. Are many Jews right in believing that the child doesn't get a soul until it is born? Were Aristotle and Aquinas right in believing that the fetus got its soul on 'quickening' between the second and third months? Or is there even such a thing as soul?

Very complicated!

When things are this complicated, you need a religious scholar.

At any rate the embryo's soul will be in good company with other unbaptized souls such as those of Abraham, Moses, Aristotle and Socrates. Jesus's mother Mary might also have been among them except that she was born without Original Sin, her Immaculate Conception. This, too, was the learned pronouncement of Pope Pius IX in the mid-19th century.

It seems that the Catholic view of immediate ensoulment has been influenced by the belief that Jesus's mother Mary, was conceived immaculately. The idea had its roots in Christian writings at least as early as the fourth century. But it was not until 1854 that Pius IX made it an official teaching of the Catholic Church. Obviously if her soul was conceived without sin, aren't all other humans conceived with a soul intact? Is that why in 1869 he declared abortion to be murder?

So, we have some questions. If God did put Adam's "original sin" into every soul, when was it put there? Aquinas wrote that it was several weeks after conception. But then we have the problem of when conception occurred. Was it the instant that the sperm entered the ovum? Was it when the fertilized ovum attached to the uterus? Since most fertilized ova do not attach but flow out of the uterus, if they have souls, where do they go? That makes the Jewish position, that there is no soul until birth, a bit more biologically believable.

SO, let's look at these areas in a bit more depth.

Before getting into the Immaculate Conception you should know something about Original Sin.

ORIGINAL SIN

"The Jews didn't have the idea of original sin. The idea that Adam 'fell' seemed to have developed after the exodus from Egypt. But it was Paul who developed the idea in Romans 5:12. "Wherefore, as by one man sin entered into the world, and death by sin; and so death passed upon all men, for that all have sinned." Then seven verses later he wrote, "For as by one man's disobedience many were made sinners." And again, in First Corinthians 15:22 he wrote, "For as in Adam all die, even so in Christ shall all be made alive." These passages can be interpreted in two ways. One is that when Adam ate the forbidden fruit all of his progeny would then be subject to sinning in some ways and to dying because Adam was no longer immortal. Or you could assume the idea that Paul may have considered, that all infants were inflicted with a sin not of their own making. Then of course they could take that first sin as a starting point and continue sinning throughout their lives. In either case the death of Jesus allowed all people everlasting life with God, if they so choose.

Some have argued that Paul meant that that first sin was inflicted by God on all humans. Some see this as unjust, would a just God do this?

Paul then popularized the idea that Jesus died to save all of the sinners since Adam. But his death and his sacrifice for the sins of humankind did not apparently wipe out any original sin that may have existed. Before the death of Jesus, were all people excluded from heaven? Were Moses, David, and Solomon excluded from heaven? Did Jesus merely show that all people could sacrifice for the Creator and therefore gain heaven?

There are some other questions. Was Jesus also conceived without sin? If so was he born totally God and not at all human?

Saint Augustine, more than 1500 years ago, was the first theologian to teach that we are all born in a state of sin. The basis of his belief is from the Bible in Genesis 3 verses 17 through 19, where Adam is described as having disobeyed God by eating the forbidden fruit of the Tree of Knowledge. So we have the first, or the 'original' sin.

The Old Testament doesn't seem to back up the idea of original sin. Some people were seen by God as good. And according to the prophets, people were responsible for their own sins, the son could not inherit a sin from his father. Here are some Biblical quotes. "The fathers shall not be put to death for the children, neither shall the children be put to death for the fathers: every man shall be put to death for his own sin." This was from Deuteronomy 24:16. And similarly, "But the children of the murderers he slew not: according unto that which is written in the book of the law of Moses, wherein the LORD commanded, saying, the fathers shall not be put to death for the children, nor the children be put to death for the fathers; but every man shall be put to death for his own sin." This was in Second Kings 14:6.

Ezekiel 18:20 echoes this idea. "The soul that sinneth, it shall die. The son shall not bear the iniquity of the father, neither shall the father bear the iniquity of the son: the righteousness of the righteous shall be upon him, and the wickedness of the wicked shall be upon him." Then he goes on to say in 33:20, "Yet ye say, the way of the Lord is not equal. O ye house of Israel, I will judge you every one after his ways." Then in Jeremiah, 31: 29 and 30, "In those days they shall say no more.

The fathers have eaten a sour grape, and the children's teeth are set on edge. But every one shall die for his own iniquity: every man that eateth the sour grape, his teeth shall be set on edge."

But Catholics claim there can be no way to escape that original sin except by believing in Jesus. Paul wrote to the Romans in Chapter 3, verse 10, "As it is written, there is none righteous, no, not one." Is it possible that Paul hadn't read the Old Testament?

Not all Christians accept the idea of original sin. The Orthodox Christians have never believed that guilt from original sin existed. By the time that Augustine's ideas were translated into Greek, in the 14th century, the Great Schism had already occurred and the Eastern Orthodox Christians were on their merry way without the hypothesized inheritance from Adam. If fact, it might be questioned as to whether the dogma of the immaculate conception is infallibly proclaimed since it was declared 16 years before the Pope decided that what he said was infallible. Was it retroactive infallibility for him, or for all previous popes?

However, there are Biblical statements in Matthew 18: 18 to 20, that allow for such infallibility, even if the Pope hadn't proclaimed it. Jesus said "Amen I say to you, whatsoever you shall bind upon earth, shall be bound also in heaven: and whatsoever you shall loose upon earth, shall be loosed also in heaven. . .Again I say to you, that if two of you shall consent upon earth, concerning anything whatsoever they shall ask, it shall be done to them by my Father who is in heaven." And again, "For where there are two or three gathered together in my name, there am I in the midst of them." So, if two members can have Christ among them and their actions will be accepted in heaven, how much stronger is it that St. Peter's spiritual descendent can determine ideas that will be affirmed in heaven?

If sin exists in the soul, and if human beings do not have souls in the first instant of their conception, they could not have sin then, either. That being the case, no one would have sin in the first instant of conception, and the doctrine of Mary's Immaculate Conception would be meaningless, since everyone would have an "immaculate conception." But since 'conception' is the key, we must all have souls at that instant when the sperm enters the ovum.

A question might be that if, according to Matthew, whether any two Christians who get together can decide things, like the morality of abortion or suicide? Matthew doesn't say that it has to be the Bishop of Rome who decides everything. And how do you think that Pope Pius IX knew about conception in 1854? I can understand that he probably knew that human sperm existed, because that had been discovered nearly 200 years earlier. But I wonder if he knew about the existence of the ovum which wasn't discovered until 1827 in Prussia. And the little publicized discovery of Dr. Martin Berry of 1843 that conception occurs when the sperm meets the ovum-- was not a well-known fact.

Actually, the Pope was probably aware of conception. He certainly knew that in the early 1780s Lazzaro Spallanzani, an Italian priest, who was also a scientist, did the first artificial insemination techniques on dogs and produced three puppies. So I would guess he had an idea of conception. And he may have known that in 1785 John Hunter did the first artificial insemination on a human and was successful. Of course, in those days they thought that it was all done by the man. He put some little fellas into the woman and they just grew.

Still today, Pope Benedict XVI's opinion is the most important for Catholics. He urges the faithful to develop a new respect for life even when it is "sick or damaged." He calls for the need to protect all human life and cites the late Pope John Paul II, who delivered the most forceful condemnation of abortion, artificial contraception, euthanasia and experimentation on human embryos. The description of "sick or damaged" life in the church's teaching refers to situations in which life is in particular need of being defended, including deformed fetuses, the severely disabled, terminally ill patients, or people in vegetative states. Benedict said that people today wrongly think that modern man is the master of life, when he is only the custodian. Life depends on God and without God, life disappears, he believed.

Evangelicals offer counter-arguments to the liberal Christians' views by appealing to various Biblical passages. Two in particular appear to imply not only ensoulment in the womb, but even before conception. In Jeremiah 1:5 we read "Before I formed you in the womb, I knew you, and before you were born, I consecrated you." And in Psalms 139: 15 and16 it says "Thou knowest me right well; my frame was not hidden from thee when I was being made in secret, intricately wrought in the depths of the earth. Thy eyes beheld my unformed substance; in thy book were written, every one of them, the days that were formed for me."

Mormons, too, believe in the pre-existence of souls. Consequently, more bodies need to be born to house those souls that God has already created.

It should therefore be obvious that aborting an embryo or fetus who is either carrying the Original Sin, that the Catholics claim, or does not have the opportunity to be saved by realizing that Jesus, as the Savior, must be understood and internalized in order for him or her to go to heaven—is clearly immoral. In fact, abortion is possibly the greatest sin. Even a murderer can ask God for forgiveness, but an aborted fetus may not have that opportunity.

CHAPTER 6 ABORTION--SOCIETAL POINT OF VIEW

Societies are often torn between what they see as a need for more children against the democratic right of a woman to control her own body and to decide if she wants to be a mother. Along this line, Norway which wants more children, has enacted laws to allow free abortion pills to those over age 16.

Russia has 500 abortions per 1000 live births. The country needs more workers, but it has not been hospitable to those immigrants who came. And, when an immigrant has a choice between the UK and Germany or Russia, it doesn't take a crystal ball to guess their choice.

The first country to reform abortion laws was the former Soviet Union in 1920. Sweden's approach to abortion is among the world's most liberal, even though abortion is not entirely decriminalized. Abortion is available on request up to 18 weeks. Australian laws vary from state to state, like in the United States. Canada has the most liberal law, allowing abortion on request. In 1988, the Canadian Supreme Court struck down the existing law ruling that disallowing abortion infringed on a woman's constitutional rights.

Rights, remember, are granted by society. People often call their desires "rights." Some would say that they get their rights from God, but such God-given rights must be approved by the society.

ABORTION IS VALUABLE FROM A SOCIETAL VIEWPOINT

There are a several major reasons for society to allow or even encourage abortions. One is to be able to limit populations that are overcrowded. Another is to protect children from being born into homes that don't want them. The financial cost to society of unwanted children goes beyond the normal societal expenses of educating their young future citizens, it often includes expenses for orphanages, increased expenses for rehabilitation from physical and mental abuse, drug rehabilitation, and increased expenses for police, judicial procedures, and prisons. So, if people want lower taxes, abortion is a major way to reduce them.

Another reason is to adhere to the wishes of girls and women who do not want to raise a child at that time. This is sometimes covered under the right to privacy, allowing a woman to make private and personal decisions about her own life. In opposition to these concerns are the questions of whether society needs more people or whether the potential person in the womb has rights superior to the person who owns the womb.

By the beginning of the 20th century, abortion was illegal or severely restricted in most countries. The restrictions were either from common law, as in the UK and its possessions, civil law as in other European countries and their possessions, and Islamic law, which was used by some Islamic countries. Where it was outlawed, it was usually because of: danger to the mother from unlicensed abortionists; it was a sin and the laws were geared to punish the sinner; or often, the life of the fetus was considered important.

While abortion was criminalized in England in 1861, it was modified in 1967 and in 1990. Ireland had a very restrictive policy, seeing the same value of life of the mother and that of the fetus. But as of 2019, abortion is now allowed in a number of situations.

Today abortion is legally permitted to save the life of the woman in 98% of world's countries. 63% of countries allow it to preserve the physical or mental health of the woman. 43% allow it in the case of rape or incest. 39% allow it if the infant is to be severely impaired. 33% allow abortion for economic or social reasons. 27% allow it when requested by the woman. The developing countries are much less likely to allow abortions than the developed countries.

But now abortion methods have become safe, if done by competent people.

HUMAN RIGHTS AND FREEDOM

The US Supreme Court has declared abortion to be a fundamental right guaranteed by the US Constitution. The landmark abortion case Roe v. Wade, decided on January 22, 1973 in favor of abortion rights, remains the law of the land. The 7-2 decision stated that the Constitution gives a guarantee of certain areas or zones of privacy, and that this right of privacy... "Is broad enough to encompass a woman's decision whether or not to terminate her pregnancy." The court thoroughly scrutinized the religious and secular history of abortion from the time of the ancient Greeks. It also found that the opinions and laws relative to abortion had become more restrictive in America as the country matured. It disagreed with this regression. In its decision, it also ruled that under the U.S. Constitution the word 'person' does not include the unborn.

In recent decades in Latin America, a combination of legislation and judicial review has lessened the restrictions to abortion.

Internationally we have some major pronouncements such as the United Nations' 1948 Universal Declaration of Human Rights, and their 1966 International Covenant on Civil and Political Rights. In Europe, we have the European Convention on Human Rights and Fundamental Freedoms. Each guarantees the rights of women. The UN also clearly states that the child has rights after being born. Some women have successfully used these lists of rights in courts to counter religious arguments against abortion.

In Africa, the Maputo Protocol (The Protocol to the African Charter on Human and Peoples' Rights on the Rights of Women in Africa) is legally binding on the 37 states that have ratified it. Included in it is the elimination of genital mutilation and the right to political equality for women. It also allowed abortion "in cases of sexual assault, rape, incest, and where the continued pregnancy endangers the mental and physical health of the mother or the life of the mother or the fetus." A year later, in 2017, African leaders went further, viewing abortion as a human right. There has been opposition by the Catholics to the abortion legalization, and by some Muslim countries to the outlawing of "female circumcision,"

FINANCIAL REASONS

Abortion reduces welfare costs to taxpayers. The Congressional Budget Office evaluated a proposed anti-abortion bill that would ban all abortions nationwide after 20 weeks of pregnancy, and found that the resulting additional births would increase the federal deficit by $225 million over nine years--due to the increased need for Medicaid coverage. Also, since many women seeking late-term abortions are economically disadvantaged, their children are likely to require welfare assistance.

Every child, wanted or unwanted, costs about $120,000 if they go to public schools. Then there are the significant police, judicial, and prison expenses for those who go wrong. The average cost of incarcerating a juvenile who has run afoul of the law is $112,000 per year.

The cost of an abortion can be free for impoverished women from some clinics, such as Planned Parenthood. Other physician performed procedures usually cost between $300 during the first trimester to $3,000 during the second trimester. Most are paid by the woman, but even if the government paid for them all, it would be far ahead financially since it would not have to pay the education or other expenses that many children and adults require of the government.

Then there is the probable economic advantage if they stay in the work force or in higher education. The society will profit if they work, especially at the higher level jobs.

POSITIVES FOR SOCIETY

Abortion reduces crime. According to a study co-written in 2001, by Freakonomics co-author Steven D. Levitt, PhD, of the University of Chicago, and John Donahue of Yale, and published in the peer-reviewed Quarterly Journal of Economics--legalized abortion has contributed significantly to recent crime reductions. About 18 years after abortion was legalized, crime rates dropped significantly. It was also found that crime rates dropped earlier in states that had previously allowed abortion. Women who did not want children were less likely to raise children who had been loved and made to feel valuable. Poorer women in areas of high crime rates might also be quite likely to avail themselves of abortion.

Studies in Canada and Australia found the same thing. However, a study in England and Wales did not bear this out for the UK. Some critics mention that the drop in crack cocaine use or better policing techniques might also explain the findings. But these uncorroborated ideas have also been criticized.

CLIMATE CHANGE AND OVERPOPULATION

Abortion is justified as a means of population control. Climate change precursors, like CO_2 and methane, are obviously increased if: there is more oil used, more cattle raised, and more concrete produced. The carbon footprint (combination of CO_2 and other greenhouse gasses) for a lifetime is increased with each child born—whether wanted or not!

Under current conditions in the United States, for instance, each child ultimately adds about 9,441 metric tons of carbon dioxide during a lifetime. Then, any children from this person, and their children, keep adding their own cumulative footprints. This makes it more and more difficult to reverse the causes of global warming, whether from those using primitive cooking fires or those driving their Rolls-Royces or flying internationally.

Climate change, as you know, is responsible for the average earth temperature rising yearly. This gives rise to an increase in forest fires--the area affected by forest fires has doubled in the last 30 years. The combination of warmer air and warming oceans increases the number and severity of hurricanes, tornados, rain storms, and snow storms because the warmer air can hold more water vapor. When the air cools, due to other factors, more water is released in the storms.

The dried hot air makes much of the land too parched to farm. This leads to famine in the equatorial areas and to reduced food production in some areas in the lower latitudes. This heat, combined with less rain, has already caused significant farming problems.

According to University of California scientists, at both Berkeley and UCLA--Florida, Texas, and California will be particularly affected. For each 1 degree Celsius increase in temperature, California's GDP will decrease by $26 billion. The precipitation, the combination of rain and snow, may be about the same, but because of the warming, much more will come as rain. The snowpack, which provides much of the water to southern California might be reduced by over 50%.

Even though abortion is often prevented, or is reduced by legal technicalities, over 55 million abortions were obtained last year worldwide. Had these not occurred, the world would suffer from more than 550 trillion metric tons more of carbon dioxide. Oh well, just turn up the air conditioner—and add some more CO_2 to the atmosphere!

Part of the Roe v Wade decision, in 1973, was "With respect to the State's important and legitimate interest in potential life, the 'compelling' point is at viability." (at pg. 164). But today, more than 40 years later--with overpopulation, climate change, and the required state expenditures on both education and other entitlements—perhaps the compelling state interest is in having fewer children born.

In Turkey in 1983, because of population growth, abortion was allowed with the consent the husband. It is allowed up to the 10th week. But now, under President Erdogan, couples are urged to have at least three children. But Turkey cannot handle all the people it now has, so Turks commonly move to Germany or other European countries. In 2017 more than 250,000 Turks emigrated. This was up 42% from the previous year. Does Turkey need more babies or more educated working adults,

TRADITION

Men with inferiority complexes can keep more "power places" available for themselves if women can be kept pregnant and in child raising. After all, that's the way it has always been!

SEPARATION OF CHURCH AND STATE

It seems that even when we have the theoretical separation between church and state, the church's theology may remain in the minds of the judges and legislators. Even atheists often carry religious assumptions with them from childhood or from the community. But fetuses have not always been so protected. Historically late term fetuses, or even infants, have not escaped the possibility that they won't see tomorrow. Subsistence economies often can't provide for every "product of passion" that pops into their financially limited world. Some societies see no need to nurture those infants who are unlikely to strongly wield a scythe or a sword for several years.. When the physical is more important than the spiritual, any manner of eugenic devices may be allowed or encouraged.

HEALTH OF THE PREGNANT WOMAN

Certainly, throughout the world there are millions of women and men who don't want to be parents. But in attempting abortion they often have to rely on unsafe methods, either because they don't have the money to afford the procedure, or the government does not allow it.

In South-central and Southeast Asia, the unsafe abortion rate is about 20 per 1,000 women of reproductive age. A lack of contraceptives, or the unavailability of abortion facilities, in rural areas are major factors contributing to the need for abortions even if they are unsafe.

An estimated 80 million women in the world have unintended or unwanted pregnancies each year. Of those, 45 to 55 million end in abortion. The World Health Organization says that there are 19 million unsafe abortions a year and that 68,000 women die from them.

In the U.S., there were 854,000 legal abortions performed last year. This is down about 40%

from ten years ago. And remember that a legal abortion is ten times less likely to cause a woman's death than if she undergoes childbirth.

THE POTENTIAL OF THE FUTURE CHILD

We might again emphasize the right of a future child, if it has any rights. To be born with the right to have an equal chance of equality of opportunity should be understood. One might assume that unwanted babies would start well behind the wanted waifs in: lacking love, financial foundations, and educational opportunities. These would then be negatives for the future of the society.

7.5 million children, one in ten in the U.S., and 2.6 million children in the UK, live with alcoholic parents. They are 6 times more likely to be abused and 3 times more likely to commit suicide.

Probably they should think of licensing parents rather than preventing births to children who will suffer

ABORTION IS NOT VALUABLE FROM A SOCIETAL VIEWPOINT

On the other side of the coin, a major reason for a society not allowing abortion is when the society needs more workers, particularly if it can't bring in temporary workers. The post-World War II Soviet Union was such a case. The Soviet Union had lost 20 million men from World War I, its civil war, and World War II.

A major reason for governments to want more children is to increase the number of workers to provide for the pensions of those who will retire. This was a stated reason for China to reverse its "one child" policy. Russia has a similar problem, since there are only two workers per retiree. The obvious solution is to increase the retirement age. Putin tried it in Russia recently-- and turned most of his countrymen against him.

Then there was the Communist dictator of Romania, Nicolae Ceausescu. He made abortion illegal saying "Anyone who avoids having children is a deserter who avoids the laws of national continuity" and declared that "the fetus is the property of the entire society." But in spite of his authoritarian legal pronouncements, the unwanted children once born were abandoned to the overflowing state orphanages. The neglect and cruelty there has been a major blot on European civilization.

When the U.S. passed the Social Security Act in 1936, the retirement age was set at 65. The average lifespan was 64—so the government made money. Now the average American lifespan is about 80, so the government is taking a financial bath! A rise in the retirement age is absolutely necessary, but the voters won't hear of it. So, governments must increase births so that there are five workers for each retiree. Then in 40 years they will need 25 workers to support those 5. Another 40 years and they will need 125 workers to support those 25. If this requirement for more children were to continue, in 100 years the U.S. population would balloon from over 300 million to over 40 billion. So, the U.S. would be the home to more than 5 times the world's present population. So where would you go on vacation? Don't worry, nuclear wars, biological weapons delivered by drones, or climate change will solve the overpopulation problem! Too bad we humans didn't tackle the problem.

The South Dakota legislature passed an anti-abortion law that bans all abortions except to save a woman's life. Even rape and incest victims were not allowed abortions. South Dakota's rape incidence has increased 1000% in forty years and is the highest rate in the 48 contiguous states, about two and a half times greater than New York's. The people, however, voted down the law. It was a question of a republican form or government, with the legislature and governor passing the law, and the direct democratic vote eliminating it. Are the people really smarter than their lawmakers? Or are they just on different tracks, with lawmakers doing what they think will get them votes and the people voting for more freedom and fewer stupid government spending escapades? But then the legislature attempted to pass a similar law again. So much for democracy-- and the will of the people!

More recently the U.S. Congress, in 'The Unborn Victims of Violence Act of 2004' made it criminal to harm an 'unborn child'. So if an assailant kills the mother, and the fetus dies, it is a double murder. If he harms the mother but kills the fetus it is a single murder. If a person causes death, pain, disfigurement, illness, or any other injury no matter how temporary it is covered by this act. However, it specifically excludes injury due to legal abortion or to injuries caused by the mother, such as from smoking, drinking or other drug use. So, mothers can harm their babies, but no one else can.

SHOULD RELIGION BE A CONCERN IN SOCIETAL DECISIONS?

Religious beliefs can often interfere with the legal rights granted by the society. For example, the religious beliefs of a pharmacist may require her to refuse to fill prescriptions that might abort a fertilized ovum. A Texas pharmacist refused to give such a drug to a rape victim. So, while the pharmacist's license is state issued and there should be a separation of church and state, the individual pharmacist's wishes can contravene the wishes of the person who wants to fill a prescription for pre- or post- intercourse contraceptives, like condoms or the 'morning after' pill.

"Over fifty years ago the American College of Obstetricians and Gynecologists defined conception as the "implantation of a fertilized ovum." This is the official legal definition in the U.S. Is it at this point that we grant "humanhood?"

We have the democratic equalitarian idea of the worth of every human being. It has eliminated capital punishment in many countries and criminalized infanticide. The question then is how far back do we push humanhood? Should it start at the voting age, primary school age, at birth, or at conception?

In the United States, for evangelicals and many other religious conservatives, preventing abortions ranks above all other social issues. They therefore have used a number of approaches to limit abortions—starting with electing like-minded politicians.

In a 2019 case the U.S. Supreme Court found that a Louisiana law that made abortion practically impossible to obtain was found to have been an abridgement of freedom. Two Catholics were in the five person majority, with the three Jews. The four dissenters were three Catholics and one Episcopalian who had been raised Catholic. So much for the separation of church and state on the Supreme Court level. (For more on this, read "Let's Look at Our Democracy," by the author.)

How is it that the embryo or fetus has no protective rights in an abortion or when its mother causes it damage by smoking or drinking, but has such rights if another party causes an injury. And how does it get any rights at all since the Supreme Court has ruled that it is not a person under the Constitution? (Roe v Wade, "the 14th Amendment does not include a fetus as a person.") I guess it's just another instance of our legislators being more psychological than logical in their thinking.

The United States aids the individual states with some funds for Medicaid. Two-thirds of the states allow the use of these funds for abortions in cases of the pregnancy that endangers the life of the mother or when the pregnancy is the result of rape or incest. The Hyde Amendment of 1976 forbids the use of Federal funds for abortion, except with these three exceptions. Only 15 states allow the use of the funds if the woman wants it—although sometimes it requires a court order.

Don't quote me, but it appears that the plusses outweigh the minuses most of the time.

CHAPTER 7 SOME IDEAS POINTING TO POSSIBLE SOLUTIONS

LET'S START WITH A GLOBAL VIEW

When we look at one issue in today's world, it is never isolated. So, abortion is directly related to the world's number one problem—overpopulation-- which causes climate change and is directly related to other problems, such as higher taxes, fewer children who are adequately loved, terrorism, and famine.

The lack of loved children is directly related to much of terrorism and crime. The fact that there are so many people in the world that are unconcerned with others, increases their tendency to violence. The number of people in the world who are deprived of a high level of education, also increases the tendency to do such things as destroying cultural artifacts, as ISIS has done in the Iraq and Syria.

Without having been loved, the basic selfish need for power needs to be expressed. The most primitive way is having "power over" someone or something through violence. We find this in every level of society in: spousal and child abuse, bullying in schools, harassment in business and the military, as well as in rape and murder.

GREATER KNOWLEDGE IS NEEDED BY LEADERS AND JUDGES

The world is much more complicated now than ever before. But the necessary knowledge needed to analyze and solve the problems is lacking in every country. How many in the American Congress, the British Parliament, or the Chinese Politburo have extensive knowledge of: psychology, sociology, history, science, ecology, economics and all of the other necessary knowledges needed in today's world?

The people are also severely lacking in their educations. In democracies, every vote counts the same. The sixth-grade dropout and the Nobel Prize winner in economics have equally weighted votes. So, their votes select their representatives. And those representatives probably gained many of their votes by making promises that can never be kept.

As long as representative democracies are peopled with poorly educated voters, as the PISA international education studies show, and as long as partisan politics retards progress in the nation and the world, we will have problems. The United States' students rank 34th in the world in the composite of math, science, and reading scores. That is two places lower than Russia, 11 lower than the UK, 28 lower than Canada, and 24 lower than China. If America is to be made great again, perhaps schools, rather stocks, should be moved to the head of the class! The saving grace is that the U.S. ranks above all the Mideast countries that took the test—however, most refuse to have their students tested.

With their lack of a comprehensive and high quality education program, is there any doubt that citizens and their legislators cannot make informed decisions about life and death? Are any of us naïve enough to believe that if ISIS or Al Qaeda had nuclear or biological weapons, that they would not use them?

THE PROBLEMS ARE COMPOUNDED

From Russia to California people want a retirement age of 65 or less. They had generally contributed enough in payroll taxes to pay them for six or seven years, but they will live another 15. Many countries allow women to retire 2 to 5 years earlier than men, because they are the weaker sex. But then they outlive the men by 2 to 3 years. So, who was weaker? Is it fair that women get six more years of retirement than the men?

In the West, freedom is held to be a necessity. There is also the feeling that we are all somehow equal. In China, the top-down principle is requiring that they have an an orderly society. Consequently, freedom is impinged. So, what is most desired?

So abortion, worldwide, should probably be looked at in terms of: the freedom of the pregnant woman to do with her life as she wishes, as well as the societal need for fewer people. Professor Pimentel, at Cornell University, the leading authority on population, says that the if the inhabitants of the world are to live at the level found in the West, the maximum population should be about 1 1/2 billion people. We are now approaching 8 billion people.

HOW MUCH FREEDOM SHOULD WE ALLOW THE INDIVIDUAL?

It is fairly simple to see that from a self-centered point of view, women should be allowed to have abortions on request. Most women will agree, many men, especially male legislators, disagree. But as pointed out above, the individual's decision can have far-reaching effects on the world.

WHAT ABOUT SOCIETIES?

From a society based point of view it depends on whether the world or the individual nation needs unwanted, possibly unloved, children. Because of overpopulation and climate change, every child born is a detriment to the society unless he or she becomes a high-level scientist, statesman or stateswoman, or is particularly valuable in some other field that the world, or the nation, needs.

How much suffering should be allowed in the world? How many unloved children should be born? To what degree should faith in a supernatural, whether monotheistic or polytheistic, be allowed to cancel the realities of the existing globalized overpopulated world?

With these facts in mind, would the world be better off if these people had been aborted?

- Hitler
- Osama bin Laden
- Abu Musab al-Zarqawi, the founder of ISIS
- John Wilkes Booth, who shot Lincoln
- Pol Pot
- Kim Jong Un
- Al Capone

Similarly, realities and probabilities seem to be beyond the intellectual capabilities of many modern voters and legislators. Power rather than progress seems to be the energetic force in our representative democracies. So, as we look at some options, we must also look at barriers to intelligent progress of our world. Are some religious beliefs antagonistic to the needs of the society?

Are lobbyists buying the votes of the legislators? To what degree does corruption increase the cost of necessary government expenses? Is climate change a real problem? And, if so, can the population be educated sufficiently to allow intelligent legislators to work to solve this costly and inconvenient problem? Relative to the abortion question--

- We need to settle the problem of having a nearly infinite number of souls born with the realities of overpopulation.
- We need to determine whether we want children born to loving parents in an accepting world, or merely that they be born somewhere.
- When babies are born in situations which are likely to lead them into criminality, poverty, or terrorism-- should society have a say in the possible outcome?
- And what about the need for workers—either on a temporary or permanent basis.

ACCEPTING WORKING IMMIGRANT—RATHER THAN ADDING TO THE NATIVE POPULATION

For the good of posterity, it would make sense for those countries who need workers to take in working immigrants temporarily from other countries, rather than to forbid abortions. However, this seldom works out well and often creates a caste system—a system with permanent social divisions. This was true in the United States and other New World countries in the days when they accepted slaves. But where the nation has a "class" system, a system that allows upward and downward movement between the social groups, in less than a century the "caste" wall can be permeated. This happened with the "out-caste" Chinese in California in the 1850s. The Chinese-

Americans are now the highest achieving ethnic group in the U.S. The Irish in the late 1800s and early 1900s were highly prejudiced against in Massachusetts. They are now the second highest achieving group of the European-Americans. Only the Poles, primarily the Polish Jews, have achieved higher.

It is highly probable that emigrants leaving an impoverished country are both more intelligent and more courageous than those they leave behind. When this is true, the accepting country may profit from the working immigrants. A recent prime example in the U.S, is Sergey Brin, one of the two developers of Google. He was born in Russia. In fact, the foreign born are 14% more likely to obtain university graduate degrees in the U.S. than are native born Americans.

The prejudice against immigrants is a common, almost universal, trait of the native populations of the world. This is a major problem with Russia, and its need for workers. It is a major reason for the rise in "populism" in the U.S. and Europe. Both the election of Donald Trump and the referendum favoring Brexit are significant recent examples, but the elections in Hungary, Poland, and Austria signal that the prejudice is widespread. Since the West is hardening in its attitude against immigrants, the baby-producing countries of southern Asia, the Mideast, Africa, and Latin America may soon be required to consider family planning as a necessary social requirement. They have an excess of bodies and don't have the financial ability to educate them all to the level that modern economies need. As the humanitarian feelings of empathy and sympathy diminish, the countries with an excess of "baby production" may be forced to provide for their own.

LIBERAL RELIGIONS

Many religions subscribe to the idea that individuals should have the freedom to control their own lives, or they recognize the needs of societies to control their populations. They might cite the Golden Rule of "Do unto others as you would have done unto you." This ethical precept is found in most religions. (Some Judeo-Christian references are: Leviticus 19:18, Matthew 7:12, Luke 6:31) But, it can also be taken as "mind your own business" or "help your neighbor to do what you would want done to yourself, such as, to complete any pregnancy with birth."

A similar passage, a parallel to the Great Commandment, is Luke 10:25-28 And one day an authority on the law stood up to put Jesus to the test. "Teacher," he asked, "what must I do to receive eternal life?" "What is written in the Law? How do you understand it?" Jesus replied. The lawyer answered, "Love the Lord your God with all your heart and with all your soul. Love him with all your strength and with all your mind.' (Deuteronomy 6:5) And, 'Love your neighbor as you love yourself." "You have answered correctly," Jesus replied. "Do that, and you will live."

This passage indicates that the love of one's neighbor is the key moral principle. In fact, nowhere in the Bible is abortion forbidden. One must jump from the Biblical passages, and the

Jewish tradition, of life starting with the first breath, to the opinions of some theologians and some popes to find opinions that forbid abortion.

AND THEN THERE ARE THE RELIGIOUS FUNDAMENTALISTS.

It is in the area of fundamentalist religions, where traditions or recent opinions, view abortion as murder, the unseen and unprovable make impenetrable walls for intelligent discourse. When neither souls nor ensoulment are provable, they are also impossible to disprove. It is the opinion versus opinion, definition versus definition, and the certainty of a pregnant woman's desire versus an unprovable opinion that creates today's great controversy.

The first Constitutional Amendment that, "Congress shall make no law respecting an establishment of religion, or prohibiting the free exercise thereof..." has evolved to the .idea of a separation of church and state.

WHAT DOES THE SUPREME COURT RULE ON CASES INVOLVING RELIGION?

The Supreme Court, depending on the leanings of the justices, has ruled several ways in freedom of religion cases. Normally they bend over backward to protect people's beliefs, but they may or may not allow certain practices. One might think that "the free exercise" of religion might allow any number of beliefs, from washing away sins with full body baptismal emersion to casting infants or virgins into a volcano or off of a cliff.

Will the justices admit their religious or non-religious beliefs? Of course not. Will they look at the three points enumerated in their unanimous, and often cited, decision in Lemon v. Kurtzman? The Court set out a three-pronged test for the constitutionality of a statute: (1) it has a primarily secular purpose; (2) its principal effect neither aids nor inhibits religion; and (3) government and religion are not excessively entangled. The statute in question dealt with whether state funds could be used for private schools.

Should secular (read societal) concerns be required when religious beliefs are fundamental to a statute even though the case does not specifically deal with religion—and its beliefs and practices?

When, in 1968 (Epperson v. Arkansas) and again in 1993 (Edwards v. Aguillard) the Court sided with science over scriptures, Genesis lost out to Darwin. Should the overpowering evidence of overpopulation and its catastrophic entrails, along with the fundamental Constitutional rights of a woman's freedom—as decided in Roe v. Wade, be sublimated to religious opinions and definitions? Abortion cases, by and large, pit non-universal definitions and opinions on "what is life" against individual freedom and the substantial benefits to society, such as: controlling population, reducing global warming, and reducing the number of unloved children.

Do the nebulous, often un-uttered, non-scriptural, opinions of some zealots reveal any secular purpose? This is required in cases involving religious beliefs and practice. (Wallace v. Jaffree --1985) And more! In hearing the unsubstantiated definitions and opinions of the anti-abortion advocates, is there any compelling state interest that requires all others to follow the mono-toned piper?

SOME OPTIONS

Until the existence of a soul, and the time of ensoulment can be empirically proven, let those who believe in a soul and ensoulment forego abortions and those who are not convinced of the ephemeral be allowed their wishes.

Leave it to the individual rather than the state. The Bill of Rights in the Constitution allows rights not reserved for the Federal government to be reserved to the people or the states. The Ninth Amendment states that: "The enumeration in the Constitution, of certain rights, shall not be construed to deny or disparage others retained by the people." And the Tenth Amendment reads, "The powers not delegated to the United States by the Constitution, nor prohibited by it to the states, are reserved to the states respectively, or to the people."

Of course, it is up to the courts, and possibly the Supreme Court to determine the issue of whether a woman has the right to choose. It did, in Roe v Wade. But with so many old male omniscient politicians knowing what was best for us--yesterday, the future of freedom may be tossed in the trash of tradition.

- ➢ We never had climate change, so it doesn't exist.
- ➢ We've never had biological warfare, so it won't happen.
- ➢ We have always had enough water, so draught will never be a problem.
- ➢ Elections have never been manipulated from afar, so it could never happen.
- ➢ No one will ever overtake America's economic power.

But things change. You know the story of the Chinese emperor who asked his wisemen to tell him something that will always be true. One said, "The sun will always rise from the east." But he had no proof. Then one said, "And this, too, will pass away." The emperor nodded in agreement.

Since having unwanted children is generally a curse on the mother, and possibly the child-- and definitely to the world, perhaps those who want to counter an individual's strong desire should pay an extra fee to support the mother and the child through the growing years and possibly through college. Perhaps they should also pay compensation to the mother whose educational objectives were hindered or whose professional advancement was slowed by the unwanted pregnancy.

It seems that the whole of society should not pay for the expenses of any child, often born in poverty, when its life may have severe negative repercussions for that society because he or she was not wanted. The "pro-life" proponents could be financially responsible for that child until it has a full-time job.

This could be a license fee, not a tax. Such a fee is paid when citizens play on a city owned golf course. Such fees are collected from people who want a driver's license, a business license, or a motor vehicle license. Such fees are paid by people who want something special beyond that paid for by taxes.

On the other hand, people in a society are often required to pay taxes to fund programs and activities they do not support. Pacifists are required to pay for wars. Non-murderers are required to pay the judicial and penal expenses of the murderers. The house-bound must pay for roads, and atheists must subsidize churches. And, people without children are required to pay for the education of the children of others. These expenditures are generally seen as necessary for the society, while driving a car or having an unwanted child are not.

HOW ABOUT LETTING THE COURTS RE-SETTLE THE ISSUES?

But what hope do we have that we can agree on the truth? In California, we go to court to settle most of our disputes. Nationally, the Supreme Court is the arbiter of last resort. If they decide on the wording and meaning of the laws, and of legislative intent, the judges will probably settle every case with a 9 to 0 decision. Why are most cases decided with a 5 to 4 count?

The problem is that judges, like all the rest of us, have their own basic assumptions. Catholics, or those raised Catholic, like Justice Gorsuch, tend to have God-based conservative male anti-abortion assumptions. Women, even the Catholics, tend to put women first. Jews tend to be liberal and oriented toward freedom. Each starts with his basic assumptions in the area being considered, then will look for court cases (case law) from the U.S., and sometimes from other countries or states. Somewhere there must be a case to back up "my" position! My starting position might be:

➤ Anti-abortion

➤ Pro business

➤ Anti-hate speech

➤ Pro climate change legislation, etc.

Occasionally the evidence will be sufficiently strong to switch a justice to another assumption. For example, in a gun rights case, the assumptions will be either societal, thinking about the safety of the population, or self-centered, being concerned about what the individual desires— often claiming a societal right to freedom. In earlier days, the emphasis in firearms cases was on the need for a well-regulated militia for the society—as the Constitution clearly states, "A well-regulated militia being necessary, the right to bear arms shall not be infringed." But recent decisions have emphasized the self-centered value of individual freedom, so the first phrase of the amendment is forgotten and the freedom of the individual is emphasized. It appears that some of the justices did not study English. The dependent clause at the beginning of the sentence qualifies and limits the independent clause that follows it. But judges, as most of the rest of us, will go to almost any lengths to find evidence for what we are trying to prove!

Looking at the millions or laws and judicial decisions, as well as the many scriptures in the various religions, and the numerous philosophical treatises throughout history—and you can find evidence for and against any legal, ethical, moral, or factual idea. Human behavior is rife with: rationalizations, lies, propaganda, non-sensical traditions, opinions—and occasionally some truths and some probable theories. We all need, as do our justices, deeper thinking on the issues rather than the simpler, and more psychologically comfortable, eternal truths that were learned at mother's knee.

In abortion cases, it is usually the God-based assumption of when life starts-- even if it has severely negative effects on the life of the mother, and likely has negative effects on the society and quite possibly on the eventual fruit of her womb--versus the self-centered assumption of a woman's right to make her own decisions about crucial factors in her own life. Her decision to abort is more likely to also be a benefit for the local and the world societies—unless the little rascal turns out to be the equal of a Jefferson, da Vinci, or Socrates!

Societal assumptions have only been legal concerns because the freedom of the individual "self" is a fundamental in American law. Should the American, or the world, society be considered? The Preamble of the Constitution emphasizes promoting "the general welfare." And while it was a reason for writing the Constitution, it has no place in the legal concerns of the judicial system. Only the articles and amendments that follow the Preamble are laws that must be followed—and they are often followed, depending on the basic assumptions of the justices.

"Legislative intent" is, or should be, a major determinant of any legal question. In terms of the Constitution, the legislative intent may be inferred from the Preamble, as well as from the notes and arguments of the Constitution's framers. But the Preamble is not law, it only points to legislative intent. However, it is sometimes cited to verify that intent.

THE CONSTITUTION—INCLUDING ITS PREAMBLE!

The Preamble may, or may not, be considered in cases involving abortion law, in terms of the intention of the writers, but it is the articles and amendments that ARE the laws. Still, let us look again the Preamble of the American Constitution, perhaps the greatest statement of the ideals for a modern society;

"We the people of the United States, in order to form a more perfect union, establish justice, insure domestic tranquility, provide for the common defense, promote the general welfare, and secure the blessings of liberty to ourselves and our posterity, do ordain and establish this Constitution for the United States of America."

In one of the first cases heard by the Supreme Court, Chisholm v Georgia (1793), two of the justices were signatories to the Constitution, the Chief Justice was a Founding Father, and the Attorney General was one the framers, and a contributor to the Federalist Papers. The case involved whether a citizen of one state could sue another state in Federal court. The 4 to 1 decision was that it could be done. However, soon afterwards, the 11th Amendment negated that opinion as a continuing precedent.

Still, the thoughts of Justices Jay and Wilson referred to the Preamble in their opinions. It was clear to these framers of our fundamental law, that the spirit of the legislative intent, as enunciated in the Preamble, be a guiding spirit in interpreting the laws.

Chief Justice Jay's opinion included this excerpt:

> "Let us now turn to the Constitution. The people therein declare that their design in establishing it comprehended six objects. 1st. To form a more perfect union. 2nd. To establish justice. 3rd. To ensure domestic tranquility. 4th. To provide for the common defence. 5th. To promote the general welfare. 6th. To secure the blessings of liberty to themselves and their posterity."

And Justice Wilson's opinion included:

> "Let a State be considered as subordinate to the People: But let every thing else be subordinate to the State. The latter part of this position is equally necessary with the former."

> "A third declared object is 'to ensure domestic tranquility.' This tranquility is most likely to be disturbed by controversies between states."

> "In order, therefore, to form a more perfect union, to establish justice, to ensure domestic tranquility, to provide for common defence, and to secure the blessings of liberty, those people, among whom were the people of Georgia, ordained and established the present Constitution. By that Constitution Legislative power is vested, Executive power is vested, Judicial power is vested."

Establishing justice, insuring domestic tranquility, and promoting the general welfare –are certainly worthwhile and necessary goals. Certainly, pregnant women who don't want to be mothers will neither be tranquil nor feel that their welfare in enhanced if they must have an unwanted child. Their time and their finances will be negatively affected for 18 or so years.

What about "our posterity?" The fact is that overpopulation and its direct effect on climate change are affecting many in the U.S. today—and will definitely affect our posterity. This concept of what is good for our posterity can override a woman's right to privacy. Should the courts look at what are the implications for our posterity in abortion rights cases.

BUT THE SUPREME COURT CAN IGNORE THE INTENT OF THE CONSTITUTION

As mentioned, having a Supreme Court that is selected by political interests, certainly weakens the checks and balances that the Constitution provided.

If the judges looked at the Constitution or the laws and looked at the legislative intent that went into forming those laws, our Supreme Court decisions would probably be 9–0 or maybe 8–1. But they are often 5–4. So one person in the country decides the constitutionality of an important issue, whether it be: abortion (Roe v Wade, 1973) by a 7–2 decision; gun control (District of Columbia v Heller, 2008) by a 5–4 decision allowing firearms as individual rights; or uncapping donations of corporations in elections (Citizens United v Federal Election Commission, 2010) by a 5–4 decision, which allowed corporations and unions to spend unlimited money in media advocacy for candidates in elections, probably indebting the Congressional recipients to favor them in legislation.

Since McDonnell v. United States (2016) by a unanimous decision, it is extremely difficult to prosecute a public official for bribery. Chief Justice Roberts' rationalization, I mean reasoning, was to prevent a "pall of potential prosecution" that could disrupt the healthy functioning of "democratic discourse." He warned that some former White House lawyers were worried that the "breathtaking expansion of public-corruption law would likely chill federal officials' interactions with the people."

McDonnell's prior conviction was vacated on the grounds that the meaning of "official act" does not include merely setting up a meeting, calling another public official, or hosting an event. If these are not official acts, I would guess that "official acts" are limited to state dinners, so the only legitimate bribery action might be asking for a second dessert!

I might remind you, that you should certainly be aware of the essential nature of bribery in a maximally functioning democracy! Heck, if the Congressional palms aren't crossed with silver, Congress would get nothing done! Looking at Congress the last several sessions, it looks like there isn't enough "green" stuffing their wallets to get them to do anything!

The Heller decision changed two centuries worth of Supreme Court decisions that generally adhered to the original Second Amendment which allowed guns for a well-regulated militia. Citizens United overturned the long line of decisions that disallowed large contributions from unions and corporations that might influence the legislators or the executives to act on behalf of the more generous donors. Lobbyists spent only $3,400,000,000 in 2018—hardly enough to sway any votes!

Senate leader Mitch McConnell received only $450,000, but there were about thirty legislators who pocketed more.

Drastically changing the meaning of the original Constitution is not new. Judges have changed the meaning of the document since the earliest days. James Madison in writing his Federalist Papers was very clear that civil laws that were passed after a citizen's action could not be used by the government in pursuing a case. These are called *ex post facto* laws. An early Supreme Court case, Calder v. Bull (1798) ruled the exact opposite of what the writers had intended, when they wrote that *ex post facto* laws applied only to criminal proceedings. Madison was very, very clear that *ex post facto* was prohibited for civil cases while bills of attainder applied to criminal cases. (To be "attained" means an act of legislature finding a person guilty of treason or felony without a trial.)

In the Calder case, a Dr. Morrison had left his estate to the Bulls in his will. However, the Calders had taken possession of the estate. A probate court gave the estate to the Calders. (My research has not been able to ascertain the relationships between the various parties.) Connecticut state law allowed 18 months to appeal. The Bulls filed late. They then asked the state legislature to change the probate court's order. This was done. In a new trial, the Bulls won. Calder then appealed citing the *ex post facto* action of the legislature.

In a unanimous decision, the Court held that the legislation was not an *ex post facto* law. The Court drew a distinction between criminal rights and "private rights," arguing that restrictions against *ex post facto* laws were not designed to protect citizens' contract rights. Justice Chase noted that while all *ex post facto* laws are retrospective, all retrospective laws are not necessarily ex post facto. Even "vested" property rights are subject to retroactive laws.

Justice Chase referred to natural law in his decision and Justice Iredell opined that "the ideas of "natural justice" are regulated by no fixed standard...the ablest and the purest men have differed upon the subject." So, both cited the ephemeral, rather than the words and meanings of the Constitution.

A number of years ago I was working for a state and it required me to contribute monthly to my retirement. When I retired I was refused a pension. The state used three reasons, not laws, to deny the pension. Another person with similar facts won in one court, I lost in another. The cases were heard by different judges during the same month. (Yes, different basic assumptions and sentiments of the judges.) Both cases were appealed as a single case. In the three years between the civil case and the appellate case, the three "reasons" were enacted into three laws by the California legislature. The Calder v Bull decision meant that laws passed after the court hearing were not *ex post facto* in a civil hearing. So I couldn't rely on Madison's reasoning. Supposedly the "due process clause" should cover such situations, but the clause "…. nor shall any State deprive any person of life, liberty, or property, without due process of law…." in the 14th Amendment, did not cover my case since neither my life, liberty, or the property that I owned were affected. After the Supreme Court denied certiorari, the newly enacted state laws were rescinded. Oh well, I should have expected the varying basic assumptions and the reality of state superiority to win the day.

While Justice Wilson, in the Chisholm case, stated his belief that the individual should be superior to the state according to the Constitution, it seldom happens in the courts. The states have huge legal teams and the ability to change laws to their advantage without being limited by the original meaning of the Constitution.

THE MEANINGS EXPRESSED BY THE CONSTITUTION'S FRAMERS ARE NOT ALWAYS FOLLOWED BY ITS JUDICIAL INTERPRETERS

The separation of powers that the writers of the Constitution desired is highly unlikely when judges are political appointees as they are in federal courts and of course, in the Supreme Court.

President Trump's Supreme Court nominee, Neil Gorsuch, in his doctoral writings and his book said "human life is fundamentally and inherently valuable." He has not said why he believes this, unless it has to do with his religion. He says that his personal philosophy will not influence is judgment. However, we might wonder about his ideas on abortion, assisted suicide, euthanasia, capital punishment, etc. He has written that "our entire political system" and our Declaration of Independence and Constitution reflect the founders' belief in "self-evident human rights and truths."

I don't know where he found this idea in the Constitution? It is in the Declaration of Independence. But a message being advocated when encouraging people to revolt is significantly different from the concepts used in forming a constitutional government. If we used Jefferson's logic from the Declaration as the soul of the guiding principles of a government we might well have a theocracy. This would be diametrically opposed to Jefferson's deistic beliefs in which a creating supernatural being would not be one bit concerned with what we little earthlings believe-- or do. You could pray your heart out, but a deistic god would neither hear, nor respond.

Amazing how we are so adept at taking a text out of its context—making a pretext for influencing others. It is certainly essential that when God doesn't point us in the right direction with revelations, we can certainly fill in the scriptural blanks with our universal knowledge—and die, if need be, for the genie we released from the bottle. Where in our scriptures is abortion definitely prohibited or capital punishment universally condemned? But five people on the Court can determine our conduct for the foreseeable future.

My favorite illustration of taking a text from its context can be seen when we say that the Bible says "there is no God." It does say this in Psalms 14:1. However, the full text is "A fool says in his heart 'there is no God.'" So, the full context is diametrically opposed to the text cited. Lawyers, judges, priests, and politicians, just like the rest of us, often do this in lying, rationalizing, creating propaganda, in their efforts to convince others.

A COMPELLING STATE INTEREST

There is a legal term "a compelling interest of the state." It is often used to subdue fundamental individual rights. It is sometimes used in cases in which an adult or a child is refusing medical care or prevention, such as a vaccination. It is also used in eminent domain cases, where the state wants property that the owners refuse to sell. It is used in the military draft and many other situations where the state believes it has a compelling interest. In the abortion question, if the state believes it needs more bodies—it can forbid abortions. But are more people needed in America, or in the world, today? In Roe v Wade, the Court did not find a compelling state interest in subduing a woman's right to privacy.

But when a state compels enough citizens to do things they object to; the people may revolt at the ballot box or with muskets or AK-47s. We can look at modern day Venezuela or Zimbabwe as examples. When women object to stringent rules against abortion, they are likely to rebel by going to a jurisdiction more favorable to their plight—like Canada, to back alley coat-hanger surgeons, or to attempt to stress their bodies with drugs, tight bindings, starvation, or exercise.

When Irish women had had enough, they succeeded in bringing a referendum to the people to repeal the 8th Amendment to their Constitution that allowed abortion only to save the life of the mother, but not in cases of rape or incest. 66.4% of the population voted for repeal, in spite of heavy Catholic opposition. As of 2019, abortions are allowed during the first trimester.

THE SUPREME COURT IS SOMETIMES TOO CONSERVATIVE

Conserving a tradition may not be in the spirit of the Constitution, or the Preamble. In Plessy v Ferguson (1896), by a 7 to1 vote the Court approved of "separate but equal" facilities for blacks and whites. Justice Harlan, the lone dissenter, wrote one of the Court's most famous opinions in his advocacy of equal rights. His oft-quoted view that "the Constitution is colorblind" might be paraphrased today as, "the Constitution is not sexist." Many believe this. The "Me, too" crusade is battling this sexist battle in the courts and in the media.

Courts continued to decide "separate but equal" cases in education and other areas for years after Plessy. While it has never been reversed by the Court, Brown v Board of Education (1954) eliminated segregated education. The Civil Rights Act of 1964 and the Voting Rights Act of the next year have solved the problem and have never been successfully challenged in the courts.

It remains to be seen whether conservative religious men on the Court will broaden their image of women from being barefoot and pregnant subservients in the kitchen to being CEOs and corporate board members, with or without children.

Regarding the idea of equality between the sexes, one might argue that if men are not required to carry a fetus for nine months, women should also not face that requirement—since "separate but equal" is no longer the national standard.

At any rate, there are strong reasons to look deeply at the effects of unwanted children, on: climate change, overpopulation, and the likelihood that the children will not be able to realize their potential, and may possibly join anti-social groups.

We can only hope that legislators and judges will look at both sides of all of the reasons for and against legalizing abortion. Perhaps the reasons can be categorized as: empirically verifiable, highly probable, questionable traditions, and highly improbable or impossible reasons. Is this too much to as in the 21st century?

Index

www.ingramcontent.com/pod-product-compliance
Lightning Source LLC
Chambersburg PA
CBHW081404280526
45788CB00009B/2986